The Hitchhikers Guide to the Great Awakening

By Ben Hawkes + Michael Dowling-Fleet

Legal Disclaimer

The Hitchhiker's Guide to the Great Awakening is an independent work of creative nonfiction and bears no connection, affiliation, or endorsement by Douglas Adams, his estate, or the publishers of The Hitchhiker's Guide to the Galaxy. This book does not reference, borrow from, or imitate the characters, settings, or narrative elements of The Hitchhiker's Guide to the Galaxy. Any similarity to names, phrases, or concepts is purely coincidental and used in a transformative and original manner in alignment with its unique themes and purpose.

The title The Hitchhiker's Guide to the Great Awakening is intended to reflect a spirit of exploration and discovery within the context of awakening and personal empowerment. It is not intended to create confusion or suggest any association with The Hitchhiker's Guide to the Galaxy series.

For any questions or concerns, please contact the authors directly at https://awakenedcoaching.life

The Hitchhikers Guide to the Great Awakening

Copyright © 2024 by Ben Hawkes and Michael Dowling-Fleet

All rights reserved. No part of this book may be reproduced, distributed, or transmitted in any form or by any means, including photocopying, recording, or other electronic or mechanical methods, without the prior written permission of the publisher, except in the case of brief quotations embodied in critical reviews and certain other non-commercial uses permitted by copyright law.

For permission requests, contact the authors via awakenedcoaching.life

This book is a work of creative nonfiction. While inspired by real events and concepts, certain elements have been fictionalised or dramatised for narrative and illustrative purposes. Any similarity to actual persons, living or dead, or actual events is purely coincidental.

Independently Published on KDP Amazon

ISBN: 9798304199032

Printed in United Kingdom

First Edition

This book is dedicated to those around us who restore our faith in the goodness and divinity of humankind,
who have the courage to speak out and do what is right in all situations.
We salute you, for we are no longer the few, we are the many.

Contents:

Notes for Safe and Appropriate Usage	1
Legal Statement	3
A Note on The Current Reality	5
Prologue: Welcome to Soul School	7
Chapter 1: Spirituality + Mind	11
Chapter 2: Finance + Commerce	41
Chapter 3: The Law	55
Chapter 4: Politics + International Relations	67
Chapter 5: War + Contention	95
Chapter 6: The Science	107
Chapter 7: Health + Nutrition	115
Chapter 8: Society	147
Chapter 9: History + Aliens	161
Epilogue: Welcome to The New Earth	183
Recommended Reading	187
Shameless Self Promotion	189

Safe and Appropriate Usage

Please do not read this book while engaged in interstellar travel of any kind, including the navigation of wormholes, event horizons and fake moon landings. If at any time you start to experience time dilations, future echoes or deja vu, you should make yourself a stiff drink and sit in a dark room until the symptoms clear.

You should not read this book while undertaking any kind of ceremony using plant medicine or holotropic breathing practices, especially underwater. If you find yourself compelled to walk around urban areas in bare feet and randomly embrace complete strangers you should continue to read; it is working as it should.

If you have recently suffered an ego or reality death you should consult your nearest conspiracy theorist before starting this book. Ask them to tell you who was behind 9/11. If the correct answer to that question does not instantly fracture your reality, then you are safe to start reading.

Legal Statement

The authors kindly request that this book and its contents are not used in any of the following ways:

- As the basis of an organised religion of any kind.
- As content in any government pamphlet on deradicalisation.
- As reading material in government internment or re-education camps.
- As research material for the writing of any kind of situation comedy.
- As serialised content in the Daily Mail, New York Times, Pravda or Die Zeitung without the express written permission, and open-mouthed disbelief of the authors/and or publishers.
- None of the contents of this book should be considered legal, financial or medical advice.
- It is provided for entertainment purposes only....

A Note on the Current Reality

The Reader currently finds themselves living in a period of time during which it will become eminently obvious that everything that we thought about the world is 100% wrong and that up is, in fact, down; left is actually right; and what we thought was light is really rather dark.

The key to success will be to check your beliefs at reception and prepare to be amazed, appalled, jarred, triggered and scared.

In that sense it is not unlike sitting down to watch anything starring Lindsay Lohan or going on holiday to France.

Bon voyage. ***Don't forget to breathe.***

Prologue:

Welcome to Soul School

This book is not intended as an authoritative, serious and exhaustive glossary of every concept, term and idea that you will need cognitive possession of to navigate the great awakening successfully. The reality is that no-one knows what the hell they are talking about. If you come across someone who maintains that they do, we recommend that you run in the opposite direction.

Absolute certainty is the bellwether of an inflexible mind. At times of epochal change the inflexible among us tend to break not bend. A willingness to allow our thoughts to coalesce and harden around belief systems sold to us by our superiors is what got us into this mess and the wise will avoid a repeat at all costs. At a time of revealing and disclosure be sure not to swap one mind prison for another. Do your own research, make up your own mind and trust your instincts.

Belief and knowing are different things. A belief is an idea that sticks around too long. A knowing is something you know to be true in your heart, whatever anyone in authority tells you. Knowing is how we know that Men cannot be Women and vice versa. It is how we know that we cannot be held responsible for the sins of our fathers (i.e., for slavery) and that shutting down gyms and leaving take-aways open in the middle of a "worldwide health crisis" are bad ideas which do not stand up to any kind of scrutiny.

At Awakened Life we hold one proposition to be self-evident; we are all eternal spiritual beings, having a physical experience and even that is up for discussion.

Question everything, remember that you are in charge of your own life and take care of your brothers and sisters.

We are all one, we are all eternal beings, we are all in this together and no-one is getting out alive. Remember to smile and remember to laugh. Soul school is a serious business, but it is also meant to be fun.

The future is bright and shining. We cannot predict what will happen, but we do know that the best way of owning the future is to shape it.

Go well, Ben and Michael.

Chapter 1:

Spirituality + Mind

If "Spirituality" puts you in mind of joss sticks, bare feet and terrible music we understand. We've been to those festivals and we weren't impressed either. The word brings with it ideas of deeply impractical people who can be taken advantage of by those with malign intent. Even worse is the concept of Spiritual Bypass which sees the spiritual individual ignore the presence and motivation of evil because they feel engaging with the darkness is to feed the darkness.

Our position is that if we are going to get into the Golden Age we are going to have to win some battles along the way. We are going to have to face evil, look it in the eye and smack it in the face.

Even the Dalai Lama understood the practical nature of spiritual warfare, but this did not take away from his deep love for his fellow humans and a concern for their welfare.

To quote ex-US Army Officer Dave Grossman: *"What if you have a capacity for violence and a deep love for your fellow citizens? Then you are a sheepdog, a warrior, someone who is walking the hero's path. Someone who can walk in the heart of darkness, into the universal human phobia, and walk out unscathed."*

That's the kind of spirituality we are talking about.

Are we all one consciousness and should be devoted to the happiness and welfare of our brothers and sisters? Yes, of course.

Does that mean we are going to allow ourselves and our kin to be taken care of by aggressive sociopaths? F**k no.

Glossary

3D:

The third dimension, representing the physical realm where we experience life through our five senses, duality and material concerns. We might think of 3D as "The Matrix". It is characterised by frequencies/vibrations of Shame, Guilt, Apathy, Grief, Fear, Desire, Anger and Pride (negative/descending frequencies) and Courage, Neutrality, Willingness and Acceptance (positive/ascending frequencies). The overwhelming majority of the population never leave this level of consciousness, but pretty soon they will have to make a decision.

4D:

The fourth dimension, often associated with the realm of thoughts, time and transition, bridges the material and spiritual. This is the realm where "spiritual warfare" takes place. It is where "Dark" and "Light" enter into contention. It is characterised by frequencies/vibrations of Reason and is a place of rationality, logic and cold analysis. Only 4% of the population reach this level (source: *Power Vs Force* by David R. Hawkins).

5D:

The fifth dimension, symbolising higher consciousness, unity, unconditional love and spiritual awakening. Dark and Light (contention and struggle) give way to frequencies/vibrations of Love, Joy, Peace and Enlightenment. This is the dimension from which most spiritual gurus will start to disappear up their own joss stick holder.

Age of Aquarius:

A period associated with collective awakening, innovation, decentralisation and a shift toward spiritual and humanitarian values being favoured over individualism and materialism, i.e., now.

Being Conscious:

An awareness of the self and surroundings, often seen as a spectrum from egoic to enlightened states. If you are "Being Conscious" then you are self-governing and regulating thoughts, actions and behaviours and not acting on triggers and impulses.

Body:

The physical vessel through which the localised consciousness housed in the soul experiences "life" and interacts with the material world. The quality of the life experience (and the ability to transcend it) is directly related to the care with which the occupant treats their "body". It is a well-known artefact of 21st-century human behaviour that the occupant will put more effort into the upkeep and maintenance of a mid-market Sports Utility Vehicle than they will their physical vessel.

Many religious belief systems have appealed to occupants to treat their vessels like a "temple". Through various translational problems and nuances over time the meaning of "temple" seems to have shifted to "theme park".

Density:

A measure of consciousness or vibrational state in the individual human, often used to describe the progression of spiritual evolution. If a human has more density, they are likely to be anchored in the 3D material realm. If they have less density they hold more light and are starting to move up into 4D/5D.

Dimension:

Levels of existence or consciousness that describe different states of being and perception, i.e., the 3rd Dimension/3D.

Disintermediation:

Removing intermediaries (e.g., organised religion or authority figures) to connect directly with divine truth/God. Also, Bitcoin vs The Banks.

Divine:

The sacred, transcendent and perfect essence of the universe and its connection to all beings. It can be thought of as an aspect of God or an integral part of God and is interchangeable/connected to/with concepts and terms such as The Field or The Quantum Field.

Download:

Receiving divine or universal wisdom through intuition, dreams or meditative states. As an example, Nikolai Tesla said openly that he did not locally originate the inspiration for his inventions, they were gifted to him from the Divine/The Field.

Akashic Records:

The location of all the knowledge of everything that ever was and ever will be is made available to us. If you can tap into a high frequency, it is possible for you to download anything you need from the Akashic Records. This is why stilling the mind using meditation is an excellent way to gain insight into anything that is troubling you. You will receive synchronicities and clues from the universe as to the way forward.

Egregore:

A collective consciousness or energy form created by a group's shared focus, belief or intention. It can be created consciously (i.e., on purpose without interference) or through programming, mind control, fear and targeted use of symbology/symbols; which explains how Taylor Swift is able to sell so many concert tickets.

Entity:

A non-physical being or consciousness, which can be benevolent, neutral or malevolent. These are generally present in 4D and are constantly interacting with our non-physical bodies. Intrusive thoughts, habitual negative behaviours and negative emotions can all be the result of non-consensual interactions with negative entities.

Evil:

Actions or intentions that stem from separation, fear or harm, often perceived as opposing divine love and unity. It is an unpopular idea, but without Evil there can be no Good and vice versa. Evil creates resistance which drives change for the better. In the words of Gandalf the White, *"everyone has their part to play"*.

Frequency:

The vibrational energy of a person, thought or environment, reflecting their state of consciousness. If someone has a high vibration we feel good around them. If someone has a low vibration their presence feels dark, dense and we avoid their company. One of Tesla's most famous quotes is: "*If you want to find the secrets of the universe, think in terms of energy, frequency and vibration.*" Everything is energy. When you get your head around that, life becomes easier to understand. You can find it in language, people say "he was on my wavelength" or talk about "the vibe". Love is a high vibration, fear and shame are the lowest of the low.

The frequency of the universe is 432 hertz. If you listen to it for 10 minutes a day you'll start to see positive changes in your life.

All music used to be tuned to 432 hertz. In the 1940s the universal standard was changed to 440 hertz. 440 hertz causes imbalance, disrupts the normal sequence of thought and disconnects the right and left brain making it more difficult to find flow state.

Different frequencies have different effects:

- 174 hertz relieves pain and tension.
- 396 hertz will drive liberation from fear and guilt.
- 432 hertz will give you a feeling of harmony and balance and can draw abundance to you.
- 528 hertz is a healing frequency and clears disease and frequency.
- 963 hertz is the frequency of God and will help you connect to source.

God:

The ultimate source of creation, unconditional love and unity; often perceived differently depending on individual belief systems. Interchangeable with Universe, Spirit, Source, Prime Source, Creator God, Supreme

Consciousness or Consciousness depending on individual belief systems and cultural context.

Human:

Pure consciousness/God made manifest in the form of a physical expression (the body) of localised consciousness housed in a soul. Hu > Hue > Colour > Light > Love + Man > Manifest i.e., Humans are God made Manifest. It is wise not to mention this concept too much around Christians. If you tell them they are a fractal of the divine they come out in a hot flush and compulsively repeat Psalm 23 until the feeling goes away.

Hollywood:

Named after the tree traditionally used to make magic wands. Hence, we get "magic of the movies" AKA Mind Control.

Great Awakening:

The collective process of breaking free from systems of control to awaken to higher consciousness. It concerns disclosure and the revealing of who we are, where we have come from, the true nature of the world we live in and the systems of control we have lived under. It coincides with the

Age of Aquarius where more localised, decentralised and "grass roots up" systems of community and societal structures are developed in response to the revelation of failings of the 'old' "top-down" matrix hierarchy.

Jupiter Rising:

Symbolising expansion, wisdom and spiritual growth, often tied to astrological shifts.

Kali Yuga:

In Hindu cosmology, the age of darkness and materialism, marked by spiritual decline before a rebirth cycle. Modern observers currently place us in the end of the Kali Yuga or the beginning of the Bronze Age.

Manifestation:

The process of turning thoughts, intentions or desires into reality by aligning with specific frequencies and taking positive action without collapse into self-doubt and self-sabotage. It is a process of thoughts and ideas becoming manifest in the physical realm and must contain some form of action or execution. It bridges the non-physical and the physical planes.

Matrix:

A highly efficient and well-constructed system which encompasses the financial system (debt slavery), the legal system (strawman/dead corporation/perpetual guilt), the media (construction of a false reality), the medical system (promotion of sickness), religion (suppression of consciousness/spirituality and promotion of guilt/shame), academia (false history/false science/materialism), education (creation of willing consumers/workers and separation from family) and many other aspects. The object of the matrix is to separate humans from spirit/soul, siphon off their energy and keep them at frequencies which make them easy to control.

> **NOTE:** The Matrix is continually improved and "built out" by those imprisoned by it. We and THEY are always "improving" it.

Meditation:

A practice of focused awareness or stillness to connect with the higher self, divine or universal consciousness. The user seeks to still the mind, focus on the breath and observe thoughts which occur and let them pass without becoming attached to them. The end result of proper meditation is stillness of mind.

Mind:

The tool or system of information gathering, perception, analysis and reasoning that processes thoughts, emotions and sensory inputs.

Mind Control:

The use of psychological or manipulative techniques to influence and control the thoughts, beliefs, emotions or behaviours of an individual or group.

We live on Planet Mind Control. From birth we are programmed by the programmed. As part of our naturally hard-wired herd instinct, we mimic what we see and who we are in the company of, i.e., "you lie with dogs and you catch fleas". If your parents were alcoholics, you may well grow up to be one too. The rise of TV (tell-lie-vision), combined with early years socialisation and 'schooling' in our education systems, provides the repetition necessary to burn behaviour patterns and thought forms into our subconscious.

This makes us prone to self-sabotaging behaviour that steers us off the path towards our own true divine powerful nature. It makes us weak, unhealthy and easier to govern. If you think you are immune to mind control then it is worth asking, why is advertising such a huge industry? Companies would not spend millions on advertising if it didn't work. There is significant negative subconscious programming in the media we consume. Films glorify violence, promiscuity, drinking alcohol, seeking revenge or playing the role of the manchild who gets stoned, is always in debt, can't hold down a job and still lives with their parents.

If you watch an important football game and your heart beats out of your chest during the penalty shootout, it is because your subconscious does not know the difference between TV and reality, and it mimics what it sees. Sport is a great way for the subconscious to feel like it has experienced competition, conflict and uprising. This is why the Romans built amphitheatres and gave free bread and wine to the plebs while they watched gladiators slaughter one another.

The COVID-19 Plandemic was an abject lesson in mind control. Repetitive messaging with inflated death figures and new "cases" were pumped into people's living rooms non-stop while they were kept locked down and inside with restricted access to recreation and sunlight. It is odd how the off licences and fast-food restaurants remained open during lockdown. We're probably just being cynical.

MK Ultra:

John Raines may not be a name that you have heard before, but he is a hero of the freedom movement. In 1971, he and other anti-Vietnam War protesters broke into government offices in Media, Pennsylvania and found documents which lifted the lid on the US government's "MK Ultra" programs. This led to a Freedom of Information Request which gave an illuminating level of disclosure as to the extent of the US intelligence community's fascination with controlling the minds of human beings. In truth, the 18,000 documents which were released were the tip of the iceberg, but the time for full transparency will come.

MK Ultra (or Monarch as it is also known) consists of 149+ projects all concerned with the business of controlling human minds and creating sub-personalities that are not aware of each other's existence. This creates all sorts of interesting possibilities (in the mind of psychopaths at least) in the fields of espionage, war, politics, entertainment and control. Popular culture (through films such as *The Bourne Supremacy* and TV series such as *Stranger Things*) has enabled soft disclosure, but many questions remain unanswered.

MK Ultra is one of the many fringe benefits the US Military-Industrial Complex enjoys as a result of Operation Paperclip, which transferred the "best and brightest" from Nazi Germany at the end of the Second World War over to the United States. For anyone wondering whether it is fact or fiction that Hollywood celebrities and music stars are created and controlled in this way, witness US singer Katy Perry stop mid-performance and say into the microphone: "Master, I'm not feeling so well".

A slightly less comic proposition is that MK Ultra borrows freely from the techniques of Luciferian practices of victim abuse and control. Indeed, it is an open secret in CIA circles that practitioners borrow heavily from the dark arts. If you think that this is a fringe activity you should be aware that the mainstream media, search engine curation, the universal use of blue light and big tech censorship are all MK Ultra techniques. In this sense we are all Jason Bourne and we are all under attack.

Religion:

Organised systems of beliefs, practices and moral codes allegedly centred around spiritual understanding and connection. Viewed from the bright side, they contain and encourage positive codes and behaviours of fairness, love for one another and self, and respect.

In the negative aspect they promote frequencies and vibrations of shame and guilt and allow for the control and vibrational suppression of large groups of people. Religions are constructed by humans and generally for political purposes. They almost always seek to place a barrier between the human and the divine (i.e., they are a mechanism for disintermediation).

Satan/Satanism:

A symbolic or spiritual archetype/belief system representing ego, separation and the shadow aspects of consciousness. It opposes creativity and life, seeks to invert the natural order of things and has provided the inspiration for millions of Halloween costumes every year.

Satanic Ritual Abuse (SRA):

Physical, sexual and psychological abuse occurring in the context of satanic or occult rituals. Endorsed and protected by high-ranking and aspiring cult members. Practices include human or animal sacrifice, the invocation of supernatural entities and other ritualistic activities.

Abuse Context:

- Victims, often children or vulnerable adults, report being subjected to extreme forms of abuse such as sexual assault, torture, mind control and forced participation in rituals.
- Survivors describe ceremonies or rituals allegedly invoking Satan or other occult figures.

Common Practices:

- Black masses or ceremonies designed to invert Christian symbols and beliefs.
- Ritualised sexual abuse or acts intended to "appease" supernatural forces.
- Animal or human sacrifice, often including children.
- Ritual sites are often places with limited public access such as country estates, underground facilities and military installations. Ley lines and known portal localities are also considered for ritual site purposes to denature the frequency of the Earth.

Psychological Manipulation:

- Survivors often report brainwashing, fear tactics or threats to ensure their silence.
- Reports sometimes include dissociative identity disorder (DID) as a result of trauma.

Links with MK Ultra Mind Control: Military, political and entertainment applications.

'Elite' Networks:

- SRA witnesses attest to large, organised satanic cults operating in secret, involving prominent community members or institutions.
- In the UK you should research "The Raines List".

Self-sabotage: The Tale of Rex and Joe

Jason Christoff is a world-renowned speaker and coach on the subject of self-sabotage and he refers to the conscious mind as a bouncer called Rex, while the subconscious mind is represented by an amiable and placid character called Joe. We have extended Christoff's allegory of Rex and Joe and how they play their part in self-sabotaging behaviours.

Imagine you're the most prestigious nightclub in the land. Everyone wants to get inside your nightclub and party and its doors are the five senses. What we can see, taste, touch, hear and smell.

Rex is our conscious decision maker. He is the prefrontal cortex of the brain. He is an incredible bouncer and it is his job to stop undesirables before they have a chance to get into the club. Rex scans everything, evaluating threats and covering every door of your five senses. However, he's not invincible. There is one door in particular, one of the senses that he is weakest at guarding, which is your vision.

Rex is smart, strategic, thinks long term, can put off immediate gratification and he only ever wants what's best for you. He preserves your reputation and helps you make sound decisions about your health, relationships, business, money, and he will not accept anyone vandalising or disrespecting the property of the nightclub/you.

Rex is the dependable adult; he represents the adult mind. He's sober, he's healthy, dependable and reliable. In summary, he's the guy you always want by your side and on your team, but his ability with vision lets him down. Any proper hypnotist knows this about Rex and will use visual cues to confuse Rex (e.g., "look into my eyes", pendulum swinging, optical illusions, finger clicking, flashes of light) so they can gain entry into the nightclub of your mind.

Because Rex is the honourable type, if he feels he is not up to the task of protecting you he will leave his post. Another way to get Rex out of the way is to poison him with drugs or toxins like junk food, sugar, caffeine, alcohol, prescription or recreational drugs. Less obvious examples include the build-up of microdoses of toxins from all the chemicals that we expose ourselves to on a daily basis, but in such small amounts that we see no apparent danger exposing ourselves to these. However, over time there's a cumulative build-up of these toxins inside our body. Sources include our cosmetic products, the fluoride in our water and toothpaste, EMF radiation, aluminium in cookware, the list is endless and after prolonged exposure all these things add up to overwhelm Rex and result in him leaving his post. When he is gone, who do you have left to guard you and your nightclub from drug dealers, pickpockets, narcissists, abusive relationships and poor decisions?

Meet Joe, your subconscious mind… things are about to get ugly.

Joe is a people pleaser. He is a DJ and loves to be popular. He loves to get on with everyone, is childish and naive, hates conflict and avoids confrontations. He just wants to have a good time and be everyone's friend. He is pain averse and is driven by a desire to please others, make discomfort go away and feel safe.

Love him or loathe him, we need him. He manages our relationship with the herd, which provides us with insurance against illness and vulnerability of all kinds. In the event we cannot provide for ourselves due to sickness, we can rely on our herd to feed us until we recover. Mankind's survival as a species is built upon teamwork and division of labour. Joe also takes care of a lot of the back-office work for us; our digestion, sex drive, aggression, breathing, but Joe is completely the opposite to Rex.

With Joe on the door it's open season for the kinds of people you would never want in your club. He's easily intimidated, highly impressionable and lets everyone in: thieves, drug dealers, drink spikers, violent power drinkers and criminal gangs.

As Joe cannot discern between the good customers and the troublemakers it's not long before chairs get broken, the carpet gets ruined and the patrons are behind the bar, helping themselves. Meanwhile the good customers (your good habits and positive character traits) have been beaten up or scared off the premises by the troublemakers.

Oblivious to the consequences of his actions, DJ Joe keeps on playing his set, which replays all the old classic songs that this new rowdy crowd love to hear.

Greatest hits include: *I'm Not Worthy, Live For Today; F**k Tomorrow, Let's Get High, The Past Is Pain, So Much Regret, How Will I Survive, Let's Get Naked* and many more.

Would this have happened on Rex's watch? Of course not.

Your subconscious is now running the show, which is typical of our daily lives where 95% of what we do in each minute of every of hour is simply running on 'autopilot' - directed by the subconscious acting out cycles of habitual behaviour. It takes eternal vigilance and massive amounts of repetition to install better habits. The controllers know this. Everything in our 3D/Matrix world (i.e., bad food, pornography, bad TV, alcohol) is designed by the dark rulers to suppress Rex and bring out Joe (see Mind Control).

Soul:

An energetic vessel/vehicle which houses a localised consciousness or fractal of infinite source (i.e., a spark of the divine). The soul is eternal, transcends physical existence and carries lessons/soul purpose across and through successive incarnations. It is a sort of metaphysical and eternal all-in-one spandex bodysuit which houses your life lessons, incarnational experiences and soul mission.

It is not to be sold, transacted with or exchanged for anything of perceived equal value. In reality it is not yours to sell, which will come as a huge relief to anyone employed in the music and film industry or the intelligence services.

Sovereign:

Recognising and embodying one's own divine authority and autonomy in life.

Spirituality:

In the positive aspect this is a personal, non-dogmatic path to explore and connect with the divine, the self and the universe. In the negative aspect it is characterised by spiritual bypass (lack of a willingness to enter into contention for the good of self and the group), the pursuit of riches without application and effort (the cult of wealth manifestation) and rebranded systems of hierarchy (competition between humans regarding levels of progress).

Starring:

A star on Hollywood Boulevard has five points and forms a pentagram. In occult practices, these points represent the elements of Earth, Wind, Fire, Water and the 'Fifth Element' nicknamed "E" for aether, which is you and your conscious life force energy. Entertainment that captivates leeches your creative spirit energy and feeds the egregor within the content you view. The term "movie" is a word magick play on words that your subconscious recognises like hidden software code: "move-e" (it moves and takes your energy or "E" so it can be fed upon). A 'star' actor is someone who is gifted at taking your attention away.

Standing in Your Power:

A state of self-awareness and true confidence, where one aligns with authentic truth and sovereignty. It is an external (generally) manifestation of the absolute certainty of one's true nature i.e., an eternal spiritual being having a physical experience.

Thought/Thinking:

The mental process of generating ideas, judgments and concepts, which can shape reality and influence frequency. This can be a conscious process (i.e., positive intentional thoughts which create positive experiences) or an unconscious/habitual process (i.e., negative thoughts which confirm negative assumptions about self and others or negative chatter driven by ego mind).

Thoughtform:

A mental or emotional energetic construct, often created by focused thought or collective belief. It can also be created through programming, mind control and targeted use of symbology/symbols, which explains how Taylor Swift is able to sell so many concert tickets.

TV Entertainment (Tell-Lie-Vision Entrainment):

There is a reason why TV productions are called Programs because there's often a hidden mind control agenda involved. The viewer of entertainment can be so captivated (captured) that their brain waves go into an alpha state (this is most people when vegging out in front of the TV). In an alpha state, the subconscious mind is very receptive to any information coming in.

As per the Tale of Rex and Joe, the subconscious has no capacity to filter information, evaluate its validity or distinguish it from reality. Hence why TV advertisements are so powerful. It's why most Hollywood studios start the film with a bright light or sun to provoke Rex to leave his post and take a shower, so their program or "movie" (see definition of *Starring*) can flood into your impressionable subconscious.

The Hermetic Principles:

The Hermetic principles are a set of philosophical and spiritual concepts attributed to Hermes Trismegistus, a legendary figure often associated with wisdom and enlightenment. They are primarily outlined in the writings of the *Kybalion* and are used to explain the nature of reality and the universe. They are as follows:

1. **The Principle of Mentalism**
   "All is mind; the universe is mental."
   Reality is shaped by consciousness. The mind is the ultimate source and basis of everything.

2. **The Principle of Correspondence**
   "As above, so below; as below, so above."
   There is harmony and correspondence between the physical, mental and spiritual realms.

3. **The Principle of Vibration**
   "Nothing rests; everything moves; everything vibrates."
   Everything in the universe is in motion, and vibration is the foundation of existence.

4. **The Principle of Polarity**
   "Everything is dual; everything has poles."
   Opposites are identical in nature, but different in

degree (e.g., hot and cold are variations of temperature).

5. **The Principle of Rhythm**

   "Everything flows, out and in; everything has its tides."

   Cycles, patterns and rhythms govern life and the universe.

6. **The Principle of Cause and Effect**

   "Every cause has its effect; every effect has its cause."

   There are no coincidences. Every action has a reaction.

7. **The Principle of Gender**

   "Gender is in everything; everything has its masculine and feminine principles."

   Creation and manifestation require the balance of masculine (active) and feminine (receptive) energies. The 7th Hermetic Principle (Universal Law) is the Law of Gender. Everything has a male and female equivalent: a masculine and a feminine. Just look at any Latin-based language for immediate evidence of this.

When the divine traits of both masculine and feminine are unified the result is creation (God's power). Creativity invokes some of the highest forms of vibration and provides the antidote to any Archon influences of our world. Hijack this special relationship between the masculine and the feminine and you are dismantling the essence of creation (and therefore God). Is it any wonder the satanic paedophiles running our 3D matrix world want to promote transgenderism on our children? Fringe benefits include lower birth rates, promiscuity on one extreme or asexuality at the other extreme. Meanwhile…

The Additional 6 Principles:

8. **The Principle of Divine Oneness**
   Everything is interconnected, forming part of the universal whole. Separation is an illusion.
9. **The Principle of Energy Exchange**
   Energy is never destroyed but transferred or transformed. You are responsible for the energy you create and interact with.
10. **The Principle of Reflection**
    Life is a mirror reflecting your inner state. Your external reality corresponds to your inner thoughts and emotions.
11. **The Principle of Manifestation**
    Thoughts and intentions create reality. Focused energy and intention bring things into existence.

12. **The Principle of Free Will**

    While universal laws guide life, individual choices and actions shape one's destiny within these laws.

13. **The Principle of Love and Harmony**

    Love is the highest vibration and fundamental force that connects everything. Harmony is achieved through love and understanding.

Chapter 2:
Finance + Commerce

If you want to trace back to one time in history, when it all really started to go wrong, you could do worse than putting your focus on the month of December in the year 1913.

This is the month and year that the Federal Reserve Act passed in the United States, which created the third privately owned central bank in US history, the Federal Reserve (which is not federal and has no reserves). What the Federal Reserve Act did, and indeed what any privately owned central bank does, is reserve the power of currency creation in the hands of an unaccountable, opaque and privately owned entity. In the case of the United States, that is entirely unconstitutional. The power to create money rests only with Congress, but why would the powers that be let a little thing like the US Constitution get in the way of the biggest scam in the history of the world? In reality, the US Constitution was replaced 42 years before, but more on that later.

The power to create currency and lend it at interest is the ring to rule them all. Nathaniel Rothschild famously said, *"Give me control of a nation's money, and I care not who makes its laws."* He didn't care because control of a nation's money gave him, and his like, the ability to buy those who make the laws and indeed, those who enforce them.

The US Dollar has lost over 90% of its spending power since the beginning of the last century. The cause of this should be obvious to anyone with a functioning brain. If you continue to create a currency, then the amount of goods and services that a unit of that currency can procure will decrease. No-one says it out loud, but this is the real cause of inflation. Price inflation may be the destination, but inflation of the money supply is the journey.

Inflation is a tax on the population in the same way that Income Tax or Value Added Tax is. They are simply unaware that their pocket is being picked. Year on year, they are put to work to pay the bill for the rampant expansion of the ponzi scheme. This will, of course, end at some point. All ponzi schemes come to an end and it is always spectacular.

The black-pilled among us maintain that this will provide the opening THEY need to bring in a Central Bank Digital Currency, which will censor our spending, limit our movement and curtail our rights. We say, this underestimates the power of the human spirit, and our God-given right to refuse when someone tries to make us do something which is manifestly *not* in our best interests.

Our controllers underestimate us at their peril. They have made it work before, but in the post-COVID world we're wise to it, and we're not buying.

Glossary

Bail In:

A more honest version of the "Bail Out," where banks simply steal their customers' money to make good the losses they have made on ever more wild and immoral types of trading and financial arbitrage (i.e., gambling).

Bail Out:

A Bail Out is a mechanism by which banks and the wider financial services industry can socialise the risk of the outlandish things they do and sell in order to make a profit. You would have thought that the ability to create value from thin air by lending it into existence would have been enough to turn a tidy profit but, over time, the geniuses in banking have thought up new and interesting ways to generate profit and destroy people's lives. The Bail Out ensures that, whatever bankers choose to do, it is always the governed (i.e., the taxed) who eventually pay the bill.

Bank:

A for-profit entity which exists to use its conversion licence to create credit from thin air and lend it as debt at a rate of interest. They do take customer deposits, but they do not like it when customers try to take them back. Their main activity is the marketing and origination of debt and the borrowing of financial instruments which they convert to credit and then lend as debt at a rate of interest.

Bonds:

A financial instrument which records that one party has lent another party money for the fulfilment of some commercial aim or other. The holder of the bond agrees to make currency available to the other party and will receive a coupon (an interest rate) in return for not having access to their currency and the nature of the risk they are taking. Types of bonds include Sovereign Bonds (currency pledged to states) and Commercial Bonds (currency pledged to corporations). Certain types of bonds, i.e., Gilts and US Treasury Bonds, are seen as "risk-free," but that was before a little thing called BRICS. The total valuation of the worldwide bond market was $140 trillion USD in 2023 compared to the $111 trillion USD worth of the worldwide stock market.

Capitalism:

The accepted definition of capitalism is a system of economic and commercial relations in which privately owned capital is applied to generate a profit. Markets move freely and price discovery is an organic and unimpeded process. That is, of course, absolute garbage. Capitalism has, over time, transitioned into an unholy mix of fascism, communism, top-down control, corruption and price fixing which exists only to drive shareholder value. The shareholders are always the same, the shareholders Vanguard, Black Rock or State Street, and no-one knows who *really* owns them.

Central Bank:

A privately owned and for-profit enterprise which creates currency from nothing and lends it to a government at interest. It is a common misconception that governments fund their activities from tax revenues. In reality, tax revenue pays the interest on the money that governments borrow from central banks. When the Federal Reserve (which is not Federal and does not have Reserves) was created in 1913, Federal Income Tax in the US was 1%. In 2024 it is between 10% and 24% depending on your income. Governments could choose to reserve the power of currency creation to themselves, yet they do not. If you are wondering why, you should refresh your memory as to the fates of Abraham Lincoln, John F. Kennedy and Muammar Gaddafi.

Consumer Debt:

A class of debt which brings together credit cards, personal loans, car loans and similar debt products. All consumer debt is created in the same way, i.e., using customers' signatures on loan documents to create credit which is converted to bank deposits using a conversion licence and lent back to them as debt at interest. If this sounds like a scam, it is because it is.

Conversion Licence:

A magic piece of paper which allows a bank to take a financial instrument given to them by a third party and change it magically into credit (expressed as a deposit in a bank account) which can then be loaned to the same third party supplying the instrument at interest as debt. This is the basis of all banking. Banks do not lend money; they borrow financial instruments (i.e., loan or mortgage contracts) from customers, magically monetise them and lend them back to the same customer at a rate of interest. They then sell the loan they have made, thereby immediately cashing in on the credit they created from nothing. If this makes banking sound like a scam, it's because it is.

Credit Score:

A financial and social control system where access to credit is strictly controlled by unaccountable private entities. Anyone who tells you that we are at risk of living in a society controlled by social credit scores should be aware that we already do. The consequences of failing to maintain a good credit score is the loss of the ability to buy a car on credit, buy a house in which to bring up your family securely and generally be a full member of "society".

Currency:

The economic energy within the current financial system is currency and not money. Currency is the means by which value is exchanged on a day-to-day basis to enable the functioning of a commercial economy. An effective currency should be accepted as a medium of exchange, and function as a unit of account and store of value.

Federal Reserve:

The Federal Reserve (which is not Federal and has no Reserves) is the third central bank of the United States. It is owned privately and is effectively independent of federal government control. The legislation required to found the bank was passed in Christmas 1913 when most Congressmen were on holiday. The lobbying effort to get the law passed involved a secret meeting in Georgia, a lot of money and arranging for the sinking of the RMS Titanic/Olympic. For the full story, read *The Creature from Jekyll Island* by G. Edward Griffin.

Government Debt:

The sum total of currency borrowed by governments from privately owned central banks to fund their spending and programmes. Government Debt is rarely paid back and only ever seems to grow over time. Proof positive that debt-backed currency is a ponzi scheme and is doomed to fail. One of the rare examples of a US President paying back the government debt in the US was Andrew Jackson, who campaigned on the slogan "Jackson and No Bank." He was able to pay back the national debt by closing the Second Bank of the United States. For this, he was subject to an attempted assassination which he foiled with a walking stick.

Insurance:

A popular scam whereby a financial institution will pledge to pay a customer an amount of currency in the event of a negative outcome such as a fire, a car crash or a customer no longer being alive. Part 1 of the scam involves the customer paying premiums which the insurance company banks and then uses them to create more currency through investment, i.e., gambling. If the negative event happens, then Part 2 of the scam begins in which the insurer does whatever they can to avoid paying the customer the promised amount in the policy. The aim of the game is to keep saying no to the customer until they either give up entirely or just die.

Mortgage:

A type of consumer debt designed to allow people to "buy" a house. The common view is that a bank lends a customer currency it already has on deposit over the long term at a rate of interest. The bank will take a charge on the property purchased with the loan to protect against non-payment. The reality is that the customer creates credit with their signature on a loan document (a type of financial instrument known as a promissory note). Unaware of the value of this, they give it to the bank who uses it (and something called a conversion licence) to create new credit. They then lend this new credit, as debt, to the customer at a rate of interest and then take a charge on the property purchased with the debt. The bank will generally sell the debt to a third party under a hidden power of attorney to ensure they are made whole from (almost) Day 1. Even though they have done this, they can still call in the asset if the customer cannot repay the mortgage. If this sounds like a scam, it's because it is.

Money:

A medium which has the ability to move value through space and time without a marked reduction in spending power. The current financial system does not operate on Money; it operates on Debt Instruments known (in the US) as Federal Reserve Notes. An example of sound money is Gold, which has lost almost none of its purchasing power over time.

Tax:

A tax is meant to be a payment given by citizens to enable a state to fulfil its part of the social contract between the governed and the government. In practice, it has become a way of harvesting economic energy from a population in order to pay the interest on the national debt which governments invariably owe to a privately owned central bank. Most people only think of Income Tax but, in the US, there are currently 97 taxes which make up the Tax Code.

The definition of "tax" can be expanded to include Fines, Court Fees and Inflation. It is a popular (and reasonable) MEME that humans live on a tax farm, and we work to pay the taxes levied on us which constitute a payment for our existence. This is, of course, a wild conspiracy and should be treated with scepticism.

Stock Market:

The stock market is a collection of markets and exchanges where the buying, selling and issuing of shares takes place. An example of an exchange is the NYSE (New York Stock Exchange). Trading is facilitated by market makers who take the opposite side of a trade so investors can exit or enter trades with minimal price fluctuation. Investors are pension funds, hedge funds, institutional investors, retail investors and many more. Stock Markets sell themselves as legitimate venues for open trading and price discovery. In the real world, insider trading is rife, especially among Members of Congress in the United States. The ex-Speaker of the House of Representatives Nancy Pelosi has a net worth of $120,000,000, an impressive figure considering that the present salary of a Member of the House of Representatives is a mere $174,000. If she banked that every one of her 38 years and didn't touch a dime (I'm playing fast and loose with the numbers here), she'd be sitting on just under

$7,000,000. Quite where the other $113,000,000 would come from is anyone's guess, but it does not seem unreasonable that having the inside track on government monetary, fiscal, defence and regulatory policy might give her a few advantages in the markets. But what would us plebs know anyway?

Tariff:

A payment charged by a country for other countries to gain access to their markets. In the world of free and open markets, i.e., elite-driven fascist kleptocracy, they have fallen out of fashion. They have recently been brought back into fashion by third-term wartime President, Donald Trump, who has mooted that he will replace Income Tax with Tariffs to drive a new Golden Age in the US (and subsequently the world?). Will he do it? Only time will tell.

Chapter 3:

The Law

The Law is one of those words that we instinctively think we grasp the meaning of.

If you ask 100 people what the law means, they will all basically say the same thing: the law is a set of rules that we all agree to live our lives by. They are all wrong. They are defining legislation, not law, and no one agreed to any of it.

In broad terms, laws are there to protect us, and legislation is there to oppress us. Laws come from common law, which comes from natural law. They are obvious statements of common sense codified and universally accepted. The law makes statements like "murder is wrong" and "we should not steal." Quite right.

In law, for there to be a crime, there has to be a victim. In legislation, that is not the case at all, which makes life very dangerous and uncertain for the common man or woman.

Legislation consists of rules that the members of an organisation must live by if they are to be functioning and welcome members of that organisation. In most countries, that organisation is not an organic nation-state at all; it is a corporation. The landmass known as the United Kingdom is currently governed (i.e., mind controlled) by a bankrupt corporation. The landmass known as the United States is in the same situation.

We are not citizens; we are members of a corporation, and thus we live our lives by pieces of legislation that control where we can go, what we can do, what we can grow, and what animals we can keep. In the case of the UK, it literally controls what we think, as seen in the case of silent prayer for unborn babies who are about to be killed.

There is a movement in the world which seeks to shine a light on this system and the evil within it. It goes by many names: Freeman on the Land, the Common Law Movement and many others. They all have common threads; those who take part know in their hearts that something is very wrong with the current state of affairs, and they all want the truth. Your authors believe that the time is now to understand who we truly are and step into that power.

As ever, the truth is in plain sight, in this case through the medium of the humble deck of playing cards. Depending on the game, you either play Aces High or Aces Low. Low, and you are the lowest of the low, the pawn that all other cards can dominate. If you play High, then you are sovereign; no other can control you or tell you what to do.

The current system is built to convince you that you are at the bottom. The reality is that, as a living, breathing man or woman of unlimited creative potential, you are in charge. The only question then is, are you willing to reclaim your birthright or continue to live in the dirt?

Glossary

Birth Certificate:

In the 3rd dimensional world, a Birth Certificate is a document that records the place of birth, date of birth, name of a newly born boy or girl and the identities and occupations of the parents. If you venture down the rabbit hole, you'll find that, though it may record the above information, its role in the commercial system is to function as a financial instrument which captures your life potential, expresses it in monetary value and bonds it within a tradeable security.

This security is then traded by government corporations and international banks. It increases in value over time until it is worth quite the tidy sum. Its value and the income stream from it make it suitable for use as collateral for borrowing. The government, whose stated purpose is to protect its citizens, uses a security created off the back of your literal life force to borrow money from international bankers, which is then used to fund rampant state expenditure, wars and huge contracts awarded to a long line of ex-ministers, ex-MPs, ex-civil servants and friends of all the above with their hands out. It is, in short, a huge scam and you are picking up the bill.

Not only are you used to underwrite the debt, you pay the interest as well. That is what taxes are for. It is not an accident that, in the United States, the act which created the Federal Reserve system of central banking and debt creation was swiftly followed by an act creating Income Tax. Someone has to pay the interest on the national debt when it falls due, and that, my friend, is you.

As with other entries, the story of your birth certificate and the sundry trusts created with your potential is too much for this book, but the pursuit of truth in this area is a quest worthy of the time and effort.

Constable:

A rank and office held in many law enforcement organisations in the world. In the United Kingdom, it is the lowest rank in a police force and the office of someone with the powers of a police officer. In times gone by, Constables swore an oath that meant something. In the present day, Constables do not swear an oath; they repeat an attestation, which is a brittle, cold and rather corporate affair that makes it plain who the enemy is. You.

Council Tax:

A protection payment paid to a local council in the United Kingdom, in return for which refuse is collected and fires are extinguished. Council Tax revenues are jealously guarded via a dark and inhuman system of courts and debt collectors. There is no legal or lawful obligation to pay Council Tax, though in practice this is rarely understood by the common man and absolutely never mentioned by the overlords.

Court:

A privately owned venue which exists to fool living men and women into thinking that they are liable for the debts of dead corporations which share their name. Popular folklore tells us that courts are places of justice, equity and common law. In reality, no court in the US has judged on a matter of common law or equity since the late 1930s. US courts (including the Supreme Court) now only judge on matters of Public Policy, i.e., legislation and the corporate rules of the corporate government of the United States. The defendant is always guilty, and the defendant always pays.

Judge:

A man or woman employed by a privately owned corporation masquerading as a court of law, who oversees the process of fooling living men and women into thinking that they are liable for the debts of dead corporations which share their name. The Judge wears a version of the Robes of Saturn to make it clear to those initiates who are aware that he is evil personified.

Local Council:

A criminal gang who run their patch through methods of racketeering and corruption. They will often approach business owners and tell them they need protection from other thugs (fellow human beings). Intimidated business owners will then share their revenues as protection money to such gangs in return for a cessation of business interruption. The gangs in turn will send tribute up through the criminal hierarchy to the Big Boss, The Don, El Padrino or Godfather.

Local Councils have taken this business model and refined it by charging exorbitant rates to businesses on their patch and harassing local residents to pay them protection money too known as Council Tax by assuring them it goes towards making the streets safer and cleaner, while closing the same streets for indeterminate lengths of time and leaving them riddled with potholes. Most UK local councils are bankrupt and cannot legally operate as corporations under bankruptcy laws. Local councils tend to attract borderline sociopaths who adore power and lack the self-awareness to accept their own limitations. What little work is done is never continued beyond 12 noon on Fridays, and many are signed off work with spurious ailments (twisted sock, nervous exhaustion) during the rest of the working week. The taxes are then sent up the chain of command as tribute to the national government, AKA bankrupt corporation.

Oath:

An unfashionable concept in modern times, which consists of a promise that the holder of a certain office makes to follow certain moral codes and place the needs of others before their own. Elected officials used to take oaths of office, but they are now more likely to be held to Codes of Professional Conduct, which allow plenty of room for corruption and contain no material consequences for transgression. One of the reasons that oaths have fallen out of fashion is that the breaking of an oath of office does, in certain circumstances, constitute treason, and we all know what the punishment for that is…

Promissory Note:

A do-it-yourself cheque or financial instrument which more enlightened and emboldened members of our society use to pay alleged tax bills and extinguish debts of all kinds. It is not admitted to readily, but it is a fact that all currency in the current debt-based system of money is underwritten by the creative energy and sweat equity of the general population. This being the case, it follows that we should be entirely capable of producing and deploying our own means of payment. We are the bank, so why shouldn't we be able to write our own cheques and demand that they be accepted? It is a fun game to beat the system with logic.

Strawman:

This is a legal concept that proposes that every living, breathing man or woman in the world has a matching avatar which acts as a legal entity capable of entering into contracts in the commercial world. It is key to understand that commerce is only concerned with contracts, and living men and women cannot enter into a contract with a corporation. If living men and women are to take part in this system of commerce (which includes buying things, being arrested, being fined, going to prison etc.) then they must have a corporate self through which to navigate the game board.

Think of Monopoly; you pick a piece to represent you and you move your piece around the board. You might be forced to pay taxes or rent, you might be given a prize of some kind, or you might be sent to jail. This playing piece is you, in the parallel universe of commerce, i.e., the world in which we live.

The intricacies of the commercial system are beyond the scope of this book, but it is a rabbit hole worth going down. Understanding it lays bare the majesty and horror of the commercial and legal matrix in which we live, and if you search long enough, you will find that there are not only snakes, but also ladders.

Treason:

The action of betraying your country. We include this definition as there seems to be a lot of it going on. For instance, if you were the leader of a country and you allowed an untested gene therapy to be used on the population of that country and it resulted in millions of injuries and deaths, would that constitute a betrayal of your country and therefore treason? If you were the CEO of a hospital in the United States and you allowed the use of ventilators on patients which you knew would end their lives prematurely because you were receiving a cash bonus for each one, would that be seen as betraying your country? No, just murder, you say? Well, there's a punishment for that too.

It is well known that former UK Prime Minister and war criminal Tony Blair amended UK treason laws in 1998 so that no government officials can face criminal charges for treasonous acts. You have to wonder what it was that he had planned....

Chapter 4:

Politics + International Relations

As the scales start to fall from your eyes, you will probably start to realise that governmental systems are not built and run for the welfare of the governed; they are built to control the governed such that they pay no more than cursory attention to the activities of those in the corridors of power.

What we witness on the daily news is nothing more than theatre. An illusion of governance designed to impress upon the viewer an illusion of freedom. Much like science, democracy has become the cornerstone of a new religion followed by those with the correct opinions. Never mind that elections rarely change anything, and never mind that state power seems to expand year on year (along with the scope and rate of taxes).

The same play-acting and wilful ignorance of true motivations are present in the area of geopolitics. On 24th

February 2022, units of the Russian Army began their "special military operation" in Ukraine. The mainstream media and the foreign policy talking heads of the rules-based international order closed ranks to send the message that this was the aggressive act of a madman who was basically "a modern day Hitler."

Never mind that the CIA-orchestrated events of 2014 in Kiev (Keev) had overthrown a democratically elected government. Never mind that NATO had moved itself east gradually since 1999 in direct contravention of promises (AKA bare-faced lies) the West had made to Russia. Never mind that an insurgency had been raging in Eastern Ukraine, gouging away at the freedoms and safety of the ethnic Russians there. Never mind that President Zelensky (an ex-actor who played the part of an ex-actor who became president in a TV series) reneged on the commitments that had been made to Russia in the Minsk Accords. Let's not mention a correlation between locations of the "special military operation" strike points and the locations of Biological Weapons Laboratories funded by the US, which had been working since then-Senator/CIA asset Barack Obama/Barry Sotoro and Deep State operator John McCain visited in 2005.

None of these verifiable facts seemed to matter in 2022, when the mainstream media spoke in one voice that Vladimir Putin was a madman and needed to be stopped, and the price in treasure (taxpayers' money) and young Ukrainian blood was worth paying.

The truth about what has happened, and what is happening in Ukraine will of course, come out in time, and it will disgust those with eyes to see and ears to hear. It will stand as a salutary lesson that when you engage with the mainstream media and politicians, you are engaging with propaganda, and the politics you thought were real were only the surface tension of the fetid swamp beneath.

Glossary

Agency:

An agency is an entity within a governmental structure with a specific mission. It is given a staff and a budget to carry out this mission. In a world that made sense, after achieving its mission, an agency would then shut down and be consigned to the history books. Of course, that has never happened in the history of the world. The nature of the state is to protect itself and to expand its power base. The human beings within it take on its mission and serve it well, protecting their place within it and the value they extract. Their loyalty is bought with a higher-than-average basic salary, good working conditions and a well-funded pension.

There are currently (i.e., pre-DOGE) 438 agencies in the US Federal Government. We can be sure that every one of them has a boss who is committed to expanding its budget, preserving its existence and never giving up its power. On one hand, we see their point. Does anyone in the US remember what life was like before the population could rely on the work of the God-fearing men and women of the *Office of Small and Disadvantaged Business Utilization*? It doesn't bear thinking about…

Anarchy:

The popular definition of anarchy is a system of governance which has no rules and, as such, descends into chaos. The true definition of anarchy is a system of governance which does have rules, but does not have rulers. Individuals create alliances, groups and working parties for the satisfaction of certain needs and generally stay out of the business of oppression and top-down control. In short, Heaven on Earth.

Budget:

A document which sets out a government's fiscal priorities, which generally means the rates of tax they intend to levy on their citizens and the amount of debt they intend on creating and then spending. For the people who read them, budgets tend to create an almost instant state of confusion, followed by a deep malaise. This is intentional, as it keeps the observer from being physically and emotionally able to pay too much attention.

Within a few weeks of a budget being published, a section of government, usually called something like *The Office of Budgetary Responsibility and Fiscal Prudence* or *Defence*

Against the Dark Arts, will announce that the budget is a work of fantasy and sophistry and that it cannot possibly work. By this point, the wider populace will have moved their gaze to something else (if they were paying attention in the first place) because the people in the telly box have stopped talking about it; which basically means it no longer exists.

Cabinet:

A group of ministers of state who come together regularly to decide on policy and the overall direction of a government. It is a venue in which real, raw political power is exercised and the fate of nations and their peoples decided.

That may well have been true at one point in time, but not any more. As an example, in the United Kingdom, Cabinet meetings are tightly controlled affairs where Cabinet Secretaries are given literal scripts by their Civil Servants/Controllers. If they divert from their lines in any way, eyebrows are raised, notes are made and the record of the event is later scrubbed clean of error.

This might seem a dysfunctional state of affairs, but it suits the Cabinet Secretaries who enjoy the extra money, the perceived power and the fact they don't actually have to make any decisions for which they will be later held accountable. The Permanent Civil Servants (the well-tailored face of the Deep State) enjoy it as they do not have to trouble themselves with the whims and opinions of horrible politicians or the even more horrible common people who they need to appeal to every 4 or 5 years.

Communism:

One of the more curious conclusions you will come to after you have taken a sober and honest look at the Russian Revolution, and communism in general, is that the ultimate ideology of the people was delivered *on spec* for, and funded by, the same New York banking interests who own the Federal Reserve.

Karl Marx was a well-funded distant member of the Rothschild family, and the travel arrangements of the leading lights of Red October (Trotsky *et al.*) were made by none other than President Roosevelt's deep state handler *"Colonel" Edward Mandell House*. The methods of repressive regimes are the same regardless of where they purport to sit on the ideological spectrum. The Russian Revolution was not run by Russians; it was run by internationalists who hated Russians. Communism was an experiment in ruthless state control, not a popular political movement, and anyone who says otherwise is just plain lying.

Controlled Opposition:

A very similar concept to the Gatekeeper. Controlled opposition is created and deployed to act as a virtual prison for those who have started to push against the mainstream narrative.

As with Gatekeepers, good examples of controlled opposition are Russell Brand and Alex Jones/Infowars. They are characterised by the use of mild exposure of secrets to protect certain groups and information which has genuine potential to overturn the power structure.

Colour Revolution:

A colour revolution is a non-violent uprising, particularly in ex-Soviet republics, such as The Rose Revolution in Georgia (2003), The Orange Revolution in Ukraine (2005) and the Tulip Revolution in Kyrgyzstan (2005). If you believe that, you'll believe that Black Lives Matter is a grassroots organic movement which grew as a result of genuine anger at racism in society, rather than a George Soros-funded Marxist activist organisation. Colour revolutions are rebranded coups d'état, dreamt up by Western intelligence agencies, to oust regimes not aligned with the agenda of the rules-based international order.

Coup d'état:

The sudden takeover of a government intended to force regime change. They are generally organised and implemented by the military or political opposition with the backing of external bad actors, such as the CIA, MI6 or Mossad. Classic examples of successful (for the deep state) coups are:

Syria (1949):
Coordinated by the CIA to ensure the continued running of the Trans-Arabian Pipeline.

Iran (1953):
A reaction to the nationalisation of the oil industry, organised by the CIA and MI6.

Dallas (1963):
Organised by the CIA, the Mafia and Mossad to protect the primacy of the Federal Reserve, safeguard US oil industry subsidies, ensure the Vietnam War continued, protect career criminal Lyndon Baines Johnson and keep the US out of the Israeli nuclear weapons programme.

The Congo (1965):

Organised by the CIA to ensure the continued supply of uranium to the United States.

Democracy:

Greek for "citizens rule," except that's not really how it works. Democracy is flawed for one simple reason: 51% of the people can tell the other 49% how they must live. In reality, it is not the 51% of citizens who rule under this system; it is the banking cartel that sits atop, beneath and around who decides who rules. For the sake of popular docility, an illusion of political polarity and choice is laid out for us to debate over, akin to a child wiggling a joystick on an arcade game while the screen flashes "Insert Coins."

Divide and Conquer:

A population control mechanism involving the use of polarising issues to divide people so they cannot unify against the true cause of their problems. The best explanation of how Divide and Conquer works is the popular meme where a King, worried by the sudden appearance of an angry mob, is reassured by his advisor: *"You don't have to fight them; you just have to convince the pitchfork people that the torch people want to take away their pitchforks."*

The easiest way to combat the Divide and Conquer strategy was suggested by author Feargus O'Connor Greenwood: you need to "cut the cake" correctly. THEY invite us to cut the cake vertically down the middle, i.e., black versus white or left versus right. That way, we remain opposed to each other and never organise. Instead, we should cut the cake horizontally and realise that it is THEY (psychopathic satanic Sabbatean-Frankists) versus the rest of us and act accordingly.

Election:

An event or "smackdown" where political opponents battle it out on TV for votes. It is like WWE, except WWE is more real, relies less on scripts and the wrestlers actually give the crowd what they want. A newly elected government is analogous to replacing the tyres on your car. The new ones gives you a slightly renewed sense of security and refreshed perception of the wheels, but weeks later you realise they're still the same old wheels spinning on the same old car.

Since political parties and their leaders are often groomed and selected well in advance in accordance with their alignment to World Economic Forum objectives, the policies and outcomes are *always* the same.

Fascism:

The intellectually lazy will label anything "right of centre" as fascist (or, in 2024, as "extreme right wing"). The classical definition of fascism is an alliance of government and corporations where the apparatus of state is controlled by a fusion of private capital and statist technocracy. So, the kind of government structure where prime ministers meet with industry leaders and the great and good at places like Davos and Bilderberg to agree on the direction of travel of the Earth and the best way to keep the people in line, then?

Gatekeepers:

A gatekeeper is a media or broadcasting operative whose job is to allow access to small secrets to protect the bigger ones. According to Feargus O'Connor Greenwood in his magnum opus, *180: Unlearn the Lies You've Been Taught to Believe*, gatekeepers are easy to spot because they never talk about who actually perpetrated the crime of 9/11 or the scam of privately owned central banks such as the Federal Reserve. Current examples of gatekeepers are Russell Brand, Alex Jones and Julian Assange.

Government:

One of the joys of taking more notice of the true nature of the world is the journey you will go on with language. In the words of Albus Dumbledore, *"words are our most inexhaustible source of magic."* Indeed, a popular refrain in free-thinking circles is, "they call it spelling because they're spells." Words hide meaning and intent in plain sight.

Government is one such word. When we hear it, we assign a simple meaning to it: a group of people with the authority to run a country. If we apply critical thinking to the word, we come up with something very different. The meaning comes in two parts: Govern = Control and Ment = Mind. What do we get? Mind Control/Mind Kontrol/MK Ultra.

It doesn't sound so fluffy now, does it? But the behaviour of those who seek to rule us starts to make a lot more sense. Commit to memory the most terrifying statement in the history of language: *"I am from the government, and I am here to help you."*

Greenwashing:

Corporate virtue signalling that enables those on LinkedIn to discuss why working for their company is so wonderful: *"because it's not about the money, we share this planet too"* or some other uplifting message. The premier exponents of greenwashing are Monsanto. In regions like India and Africa, Monsanto has promoted GM seeds as a solution to hunger and low crop yields. The reality is that smallholders are pushed into debt as they struggle to afford the basic supplies their profession requires. This generally results in business failure and suicide. How uplifting.

Hegelian Dialectic:

A philosophical framework developed by German philosopher Georg Wilhelm Friedrich Hegel. It describes the process of development of ideas or concepts (or societal phenomena) through a three-step progression: thesis, antithesis and synthesis. A more useful way of describing the 3-step process is Problem, Reaction, Solution. This might play out as follows:

1. **Problem:** Islamist terrorists have flown some airplanes into the World Trade Center Towers 1 and 2, the Pentagon and a field in Pennsylvania, killing a lot of innocent people.
2. **Reaction:** The people of the United States demand the head of Osama Bin Laden, a domestic crackdown on terrorists and "War On Terror".

3. **Solution:** Use the Patriot Act to expand the surveillance state and then launch several ruinous wars in the desert, which will make lots of money for the Defence-Industrial Complex and politically achieve precisely nothing.

The Hegelian Dialectic can play out over years, decades or centuries. THEY are very patient and are happy to play the long game.

Ideology:

A system of ideas, beliefs, values or principles that shapes how individuals and groups view the world. In other words, it is a framework of thought (mind control programming) that often falsely explains how the world works as an ideal concept.

Examples of ideologies:

Political:
Democracy, socialism, authoritarianism (basically different names for the same way of controlling the population).

Economic:
Free-market capitalism, Keynesian economics, communism (again, different names, but the same outcome).

Cultural/Social:

Nationalism, secularism, multiculturalism (all deflect from the true nature and divine power of the individual).

Religious:

Christianity, Islamism and atheism as frameworks for interpreting the world (all forms of restricted 'mediation' between the people and their divine source).

Some ideologies develop over time from a basis of organic human interaction and thought (i.e., non-US liberalism and conservatism). Others (i.e., communism) are entirely synthetic sets of ideas created to order for the elites by "bought and paid for" agents of those elites (i.e., Karl Marx).

Incompetency:

The standard argument used to explain away malevolent government policies, i.e., "no, they're not evil, they're just stupid." This sort of logic is well used by the more "radical" fringes of the Alt-Right, such as *The Daily Sceptic* and *Triggernometry* in the UK, and sometimes by Joe Rogan in the United States. The incompetency stereotype ensures that the public never suspect that those in control plan in 500-year blocks and are quite happy to arrange or allow the genocide of entire peoples to further the achievement of a policy goal.

Interest Group:

An entity or group of entities that coalesce around a political or social issue or product/industry, which the enfeebled minds of the general public might be opposed to if they were aware of the reality of it. By far the most powerful interest group in the United States is AIPAC, the American Israel Public Affairs Committee, which exists to further the interests of Israel and the Zionist project in the US government. AIPAC does not fund politicians directly but instead funds Political Action Committees (PACs), which exist to support individual politicians. AIPAC funds them to the tune of several million per PAC. One wonders what it is that they ask for in return for all that money...

International Rules Based Order:

A group of democratic countries who respect the sovereignty of other nation states and base their decisions on adherence to international law and morality. They claim to believe in the restraint of military force, respect for the democratic process in other countries, and strong international institutions that maintain order and transparency in the affairs of nations.

In reality, this is one of those terms that means the exact opposite of what it seems. The International Rules Based

Order runs on child trafficking, money laundering, illegal arms deals and relentless interference in the affairs of other nations. It specialises in regime change, ruinous wars in countries in which they have no legitimate interest and leaving countries "better than they found them," i.e., with a central bank and all oil concessions in the hands of US Blue Chip companies.

At the time of writing (December 2024), they are currently focussed on Syria, Romania and Georgia; all countries which have either elected a leader who doesn't want to play the game or have a leader who has realised that the United States funds terrorism in the Middle East as a means of destabilising the region. To answer the question building in your mind as you read this: no, we are not the good guys.

Israel:

A deep state theme park located in the Middle East/Levant. It is famous for its aggressive property development policies in the Gaza Strip, sense of spiritual entitlement, and unapologetic influence over US politics and genocide.

Liberal:

A classic liberal believes in free speech and the rights of the individual to live free and happy, away from the prying eyes of government. A modern mutated liberal believes that the government exists to protect them from being offended because their unrelenting status anxiety is readily abated by assigning themselves 'unique' (banal) social labels, which they pin on their social blazer lapel like club badges. This is all in aid of masking their true inner sense of mediocrity and unremarkableness. This results in modern liberals pouncing on anything that provides an air of non-conformity (mostly superficial) or appearing "controversial" (the easily triggered love to pull triggers). As such, there is a predisposition to "over egging the omelette" about any issue they feel may polarise or trigger a reaction from the "savages" in their midst. Seeking provocation is a pastime for Liberals with chips on their shoulders. Examples include, making a 'statement' about being lesbian or mixed race or maintaining that reproductive rights is the most important human rights issue of the day. They must have a label, and they must have a cause (they need a sense of purpose). The Daffyd Thomas character of the UK TV comedy Little Britain, demonstrated such status anxiety to great comedic effect.

Modern liberals are best avoided, and nowadays you can see them coming from a long way off because their hair is typically pink and they often come into work dressed like they just fell out of bed.

Beware "liberals-in-waiting", mostly personified by pseudo-middle-class personas. Thankfully, they are increasingly rare, as they are mostly ageing Baby Boomers who live in gated communities where they can safely express, but not embody, luxury beliefs about electric cars, immigration, transgenderism and monetarism while sipping on an espresso and scrolling through their iPads.

This kind of liberal sincerely believes that any other political ideology is populist fascism reserved for the plebs. You should expect a penchant for broadsheet newspapers like *The Telegraph* (or *The Washington Post*), an overwhelming belief in the BBC (or CNN) as a morally principled institution with a dedication to the "truth." These liberals-in-waiting measure their intelligence by their ability to parrot narratives, pronounce the word "carpaccio" correctly and always have a refillable water bottle about their person.

Tory Boy:

Typically, a grammar school 'nouveau' type from England (usually the South East) who wishes he attended a traditional Public School (e.g., Eton, Harrow, Charterhouse, Sherbourne).

"All 11 Plus and no Common Entrance" means this poor chap suffers constant status anxiety and lusts after the acceptance of the old money crowd. This is what makes Tory Boy so dangerous. He's vulnerable to flattery and influence by Davos types and readily compromised when working in public affairs or public office.

Symptoms include mandatory voting for Conservatives (and signalling his vote at every opportunity); general social climbing and sycophantic behaviour; regurgitating sound bytes from The Financial Times, BBC or World Economic Forum.

Last seen holding a glass of Pimms, mincing at the Henley Regatta (just listen for the fake over-the-top laughter). Just don't mention The Member's Enclosure at Wimbledon, he's not been invited yet (how beastly of them).

Limited Hangout:

An ideological or cognitive virtual prison created to ensure that mild disclosure does not become full disclosure.

Good examples of Limited Hangouts are Aliens and 9/11. With Aliens, the existence of space programmes, alien technology and the existence of aliens are used as a barrier to a more significant truth: that humanity has probably had formalised relations with aliens for quite some time. With 9/11, a shield narrative (that 9/11 was a false flag arranged by Neo-Con insiders to further commercial and political interests) is used to hide the wider truth: that it was planned and implemented by Mossad/Israel.

Anti-Semitic tropes ("the Jews did it!") are used in this way to muddy these waters and hide the identities of the true protagonists (Sabbatean-Frankists). The term "Anti-Semitic" is, in itself, a limited hangout, as Jewish people are generally not Semites. Go figure.

Lobbyist:

An individual political operator who works to further the cause of any number of interest groups. The best place to gain insight into the work of a lobbyist is the 2006 film, *Thank You for Smoking*.

Manifesto:

A sales brochure used by a political party which sets out the features, advantages and benefits of voting for them to form a government rather than someone else.

A manifesto is usually the work of delusional and sleep-deprived junior political advisors. Political parties love manifestos because they know they will never be held to the promises within them. If this state of affairs were repeated in any field of commerce, it would result in legal action and acute financial woe for the maker of the broken promises. Because it is politics, these things are memory-holed and never spoken about again in polite society.

NGO:

A Non-Governmental Organisation used to mean an organisation such as *Save the Children* or *The World Wildlife Fund*, which had generally benign aims and focused on problems which genuinely needed to be solved.

In recent years, we have seen the rise of other kinds of organisations, which exist to redeploy the ill-gotten gains of obvious sociopaths such as George Soros to exploit divisive social issues to hasten the process of societal demoralisation, degradation and decay. These organisations go by reasonable names such as *The Open Societies Foundation*, *The Vaccine Alliance* and *Death to All the Free Peoples of the Earth* (sic).

The Controllers enjoy the use of NGOs as they can walk the corridors of (pretend) power with impunity because they wear such moral clothes. Some NGOs, such as *The Clinton Foundation*, have long since stopped bothering with the charade and simply concentrate their efforts entirely on child trafficking and money laundering.

Not For Profit/Foundation:

Politicians, bad actors, dark players, or more simply arseholes, love getting involved with these because of the following reasons:

1. Lack of transparency or accountability
2. Lucrative salaries for directors with bloated expenses
3. Tax avoidance
4. Self-serving goals, ideologies and hidden agendas cloaked in virtue signalling or "greenwashing" (see definition)
5. Opaque sources of funding (it's probably Gates, Soros, Rockefellers, Rothschilds et al. anyway)
6. Frontrunning investments off the back of huge endowments
7. Almost zero regulation
8. Exploitation of staff and volunteers
9. Exploitation of the people in the very communities these foundations purport to help (*Oxfam* in Haiti)
10. Wealthy donors can make decisions for entire communities without consulting them (see *Bill and Melinda Gates Foundation*)
11. One-size-fits-all "One World Government" approach without regard for cultural or local differences

In 2018, *Oxfam* was revealed for sexual misconduct by its staff during the 2010 Haiti earthquake relief efforts (see *Clinton Foundation* because they had a good time in Haiti too). An internal investigation in 2011 uncovered that senior staff members, including the country director, Roland Van Hauwermeiren, engaged in sexual exploitation, such as hiring prostitutes, some of whom were underage (see a pattern?). The investigation also highlighted a "culture of impunity" among the staff involved.

Nationalism:

In globalist circles, nationalism is a very dirty word. It speaks of national pride and patriotism, which makes it very difficult for the deep state to ensure that populations are docile and easy to manage. It is only one step on the emotional frequency chart from Pride to Courage. A general outbreak of Courage in a national population would be very bad news indeed and is to be avoided at all costs.

This is why the mainstream media and political classes do whatever they can, whenever they can, as much as they can, to equate nationalism and patriotism with extreme right-wing white supremacy. It is, of course, OK to take pride in your ethnic background if you are not British or American.

Opposition:

The opposition consists of those political parties not currently in power. Their apparent job is to fight the governing party tooth and nail on all matters and hold them to account for their conduct, decisions and general governance.

In reality, they all work for the same people, are working towards the same policy objectives/narratives/plot lines and went to the same universities. The illusion of opposition is a fundamental building block of "democracy," which seeks to show that there are inbuilt controls in the system to protect people's rights.

This is, of course, garbage, as the conduct of the "loyal opposition," the Labour Party, showed in Spring 2020. While the government formed by the Conservative Party was merrily destroying the economic and social fabric of the United Kingdom with lockdowns, the Labour Party were holding them to account by arguing that they should have locked down earlier, harder and for longer. It is, of course, all theatre.

Republic:

A political entity which operates as a representative democracy, ensures that no one is above the law and that individual rights are protected.

The United States is officially a republic, but in practice, it functions as a corporate government which operates to further state power, provide financial enrichment to those closest to the central bank money spigot and suppress free speech and individual rights so that no one is able to organise and oppose their criminal government.

The rumour is that Donald Trump restored the Republic during his first term, and the chaos we have seen since then is a consequence of the fall of the corporate government installed in 1871. We shall see.

Chapter 5:

War + Contention

The Business of War:

The total mobilisation of a nation's resources to achieve the subjugation of a competitor nation is not a natural state of affairs. Given that we are all parts of the same consciousness, and therefore all brothers and sisters, it doesn't make any sense that we should spend our time and resources trying to un-alive each other. German and British soldiers came to this conclusion during Christmas 1914, and the Generals were rather cross about it.

This inescapable reality (of brotherhood and sisterhood) means that THEY need to go to all sorts of trouble to get us to shoot at each other. THEY have become very good at this over time. Events such as *The Gulf of Tonkin* (Vietnam War), *RMS Lusitania* (World War 1), and *Weapons of Mass*

Destruction (Gulf War 2) were all set-ups designed to inflame tensions and provide a pretext for war.

So why do our controllers adore war so much? As with any of their activities, it achieves many outcomes in one hit.

1 - War is a Racket:

General Smedley Butler, a decorated US Marine Corps General, famously admitted this in a speech after he left the service. All wars have a commercial element; at its core, war is armed robbery writ large, designed to take and hold resources that an aggressor would not normally have access to. For example, the Second Gulf War was a huge payday for the US oil and infrastructure industry. They gained access to markets they did not have before and cashed in with relative ease.

2 - All Wars are Bankers' Wars:

It is an article of faith for the international bankers that they adore war because they can lend to both sides. They make money from the victors (interest payments and market access) and the losers (leverage and national assets bought for cents on the dollar). It is famously said that the British Royal Family lost their rights to expand their family as they wished, to the Rothschild Family, due to the crippling financial situation they found themselves in after the First World War.

It is also now known that the United States had a corporate governmental structure and bankruptcy forced on them by their creditors when they could not roll over their Civil War Debt. This led to the Constitution of 1871 and the fall of the Republic. This is not well known, but if you know where to look, you will find the proof.

3 - Access to Birth Certificate Trusts:

Widespread death in the general population is a payday for any government since the late 1600s. It allows the State full access to the value within a citizen's Birth Certificate Trust. This is why soldiers are made to carry Dog Tags so they can be identified after death. No identification and confirmation of death? No trust access.

4 - Ritual Sacrifice and Desecration:

This one is a little hard to take, so I will just go ahead and say it. Wars are ideal opportunities for those behind our governments to arrange for the sacrifice of large amounts of humans and harvest energy from the process.

Would it surprise you to know that the Battle of Kursk in 1943, the largest tank battle in the history of the world, took place on the crossing point of several major ley lines? When you realise that human energy is highly prized by THEY, it doesn't seem like much of a coincidence.

You should also factor in that during the Second World War, beautiful cities (with no military value) such as Dresden, Norwich, Bath, Canterbury, Exeter and Lubeck were razed to the ground by the RAF and Luftwaffe. The destruction of beautiful architecture and old-world buildings fulfils a purpose for the controllers. They are an attack not only on a country's housing stock but also on their spirit and soul.

Thankfully, war will very soon be out of fashion, but unless we understand the past, we are doomed to repeat it.

Glossary

9/11:

On 11th September, World Trade Centre Towers 1, 2 and 7 were destroyed, and the Pentagon was attacked. The official story is that four planes were hijacked and used as weapons by Al Qaeda terrorists in a plan coordinated and planned by Osama Bin Laden. WTCs 1 and 2 fell early in the day, and WTC 7 in the late afternoon, allegedly as a result of fires caused by office furniture.

There are numerous holes in the official version of events and many questions that remain unanswered. A full rundown of the events of that day is beyond the scope of this book, but we should all be aware of at least the following:

1. Almost all physical evidence was removed from the attack site without being examined properly.
2. There were high amounts of radioactive material at the attack site.
3. No modern skyscraper has been toppled by fire, either before or since.

4. First responders reported the sounds of demolition charges being used in WTC 1, 2 and 7.
5. The flight path of both airplanes allegedly used was, in human and aerodynamic terms, impossible.
6. It was not possible for fire caused by jet fuel to melt the beams used to construct the towers.
7. All three towers collapsed into their own footprint at free-fall speed, i.e., unimpeded.

A common meme is that "9/11 was an inside job." That is a limited hangout. It was not an inside job, it was an outside job. Can you guess who did it?

Conspiracy/Conspiracy Theory:

A secret plan or agreement between two or more individuals to commit an unlawful, harmful or deceitful act. The term is often used to describe covert actions undertaken by individuals or groups to achieve a specific agenda, typically to gain power, influence or control, while keeping the plan hidden from public awareness.

- The term "conspiracy theory" is often used pejoratively to dismiss and delegitimise critics.
- Emphasis is placed on the complexity and implausibility of conspiracy theories, suggesting that such ideas require too many people to remain silent.

- It encourages the idea that belief in conspiracy theories stems from paranoia or a lack of understanding of reality.

The term "conspiracy theory" in public consciousness has become a dismissive label for scepticism or dissent, regardless of its validity. Over time, the phrase has come to imply baseless speculation, discouraging critical inquiry into controversial events. It is well known that the term "Conspiracy Theory was invented by the CIA to limit skeptical comment on the findings of the Warren Commission after the ritual murder of President John F. Kennedy.

False Flag:

An operation, usually involving significant loss of life, which is designed to appear as if a certain group is responsible for it, rather than the actual perpetrators.

A false flag is generally designed to provide the trigger for a wider conflict that would not be possible without the false flag. A good example of a false flag operation is 9/11.

The operational concept behind the events of 9/11 is still hotly contested. Manifestly, the damage caused was not possible *via* the means that the official report proposed. The cause of the destruction of the three towers which fell was certainly a prepared demolition of some kind. The nature of the means of demolition is unclear and could have been thermite, miniature nuclear weapons, directed energy weapons or a mixture of all three.

The Pentagon attack was likely to have been effected using a cruise missile of some sort; the damage caused would not have been possible using a civilian airplane. It allegedly involved Al Qaeda and Osama Bin Laden, both of whom were CIA creations.

9/11 was a multi-layered crime that stands as one of the greatest criminal acts in modernity. It involved:

1. The murder of thousands of innocent people on the day.
2. The long-range deaths from cancer of thousands more first responders and residents.
3. Countless civilian lives lost in Iraq.
4. The deaths of military personnel from many countries who risked their lives in good faith.

9/11 was a political operation, an insurance scam, a bond scam, a trading scam and a geopolitical crime designed to increase the surveillance state and enrich the military-industrial complex for many years to come. In that sense, it worked perfectly.

Intelligence Agency:

A job creation programme for those with high intelligence and incurable sociopathy.

A fine example of an intelligence agency with a healthy sense of mission is the US Central Intelligence Agency (CIA), which operates from Langley in Virginia. Known as "The Company" by cult members, it specialises in extortion, drug running, child trafficking and, occasionally, collecting and analysing intelligence to be used by the US government when making political, geopolitical and military decisions.

JFK famously said that he would "splinter the CIA into a thousand pieces and scatter it to the winds." Soon after, he was murdered in a ritual sacrifice operation in Dallas, Texas, by a loose alliance of bad actors, including…the CIA. It is a matter of fact that future Director of Central Intelligence and President of the United States George H. Bush was in Dallas that day, though he professed not to remember much about it all.

Lusitania:

The RMS *Lusitania* was a British passenger ship sunk by a German U-Boat off the coast of Southern Ireland in May 1915. It was a key event in the decision by the US to enter the First World War on the side of Great Britain, France and Russia.

There are many questions still to be answered about the circumstances of the sinking, and many facts concerning it are still classified by the UK government.

What we do know:

1. Winston Churchill (then First Sea Lord) was instrumental in creating the preconditions for the sinking by giving an order that stripped the *Lusitania* of her naval escorts.
2. The *Lusitania* was carrying arms and ammunition (illegally) and, as such, was a legitimate military target.
3. 1,198 souls lost their lives that night, and THEY got what they wanted: the United States entered the war on 6th April 1917.

A large influence on the decision was the outcry at the loss of American life in the sinking.

Military-Industrial Complex:

An unholy alliance of defence contractors, government, intelligence agencies, consultancies, think tanks and more, who together have provided the pretext, political momentum and material for almost all wars in modernity.

Outgoing US President Dwight D. Eisenhower famously said in 1961:

> *"We must guard against the acquisition of unwarranted influence, whether sought or unsought, by the military-industrial complex. The potential for the disastrous rise of misplaced power exists and will persist."*

The next President, John F. Kennedy, did indeed try to guard against the unwarranted influence of the Defence-Industrial Complex, and it cost him his life.

Terrorism:

The use of organised and semi-organised terror events or narratives to achieve a political end.

Traditionally, terrorism has been a state activity, with its target being the people. In the late 20th century and early 21st century, terrorism seemed to become an activity undertaken by groups seeking to influence state policy from the outside. On closer inspection, it turned out it was still the government, only this time they were dressed as Arabs.

In the present day, terrorism is again almost exclusively a state activity (see Chemtrails, Vaccines and Israel).

Chapter 6:

The Science

In the western world, religion is out of fashion. It is thought of as frightfully passé to believe in something that you cannot see. In 2024, if Moses had posted on X that he had seen God, the likely response from the majority of commenters would probably be, "Source?" The irony of the choice of nomenclature is not lost on us. *Source* or *Universe* or *God*. It's all the same thing.

In the absence of something to believe in, the educated and professional classes have happened upon "The Science" as a reasonable replacement for belief in something bigger than oneself. "The Science" is a place of rules, proof and certainty. In deeply confusing times, it is a refuge for those unable to accept that uncertainty is the only certainty. "The Science" is a place where brittle minds find comfort.

On the other hand, *science* (the business of rational and honest scientific inquiry) is a place for lively and enquiring minds to ask questions, slay dragons (which did exist) and show that the emperor is, in fact, stark bollock naked!

The Great Awakening will not be kind to every man or woman in a white coat, but for those willing to start the day with an open mind, all sorts of wonders await. Zero Point Technology, the Ontological Model of Reality, Remote Viewing, Telekinesis and more all await as legitimate venues for scientific enquiry.

In short, if you are a scientist, there is no better time to be alive, but only if you are willing to admit that we were wrong about almost everything…

Glossary

Carbon Dioxide:

The "gas of life" that sustains plant life, but is somehow simultaneously also capable of killing every living thing on the planet in a ball of infernal fire.

Chemtrails:

An activity involving the spraying of barium, heavy metals, or fly ash in the sky by specially modified aeroplanes. Chemtrail spotting has become a popular hobby in the 2020s. The goal of the activity is to reduce the health and cognitive ability of a population so that they can be more easily controlled and made better repeat customers for the Pharma-Industrial Complex.

Climate Change:

Propagated as being anthropogenic in origin (man-made and by bovine flatulence), not to be confused with *Weather Manipulation*.

Originally termed *Global Warming*, but since the Earth, if anything, has actually got cooler over the past 40 years, it has evolved into *Climate Change* to encompass all climate outcomes. In 1990, it was modelled that the North Pole would melt and much of the world's coastline would be underwater. This did not happen. It was prophesied and modelled using university research that by 2015, the same thing would occur: it didn't.

The beachside properties of Camp Cove in Sydney Harbour are all still above water, property prices in similar situations continue to rise and, more tellingly, are still financed and insured. Meanwhile, there's a tax on vehicles for carbon emissions, on air travel and almost anything else you can think of.

Consider Australia's contribution to global fossil fuel-burning carbon dioxide emissions:

1. 0.04% of the Earth's atmosphere is carbon dioxide, of which all the countries in the world combined contribute 3% of this 0.04%.
2. Australia is accountable for 1.3% of the 3% of the 0.04%.

To illustrate: if the Earth's atmosphere were £1,000,000, all the carbon dioxide would amount to £400. Out of that £400, fossil fuel burning by every country on Earth would contribute £12. Australia's contribution to that £12 would be just 15.6 pence.

Yet, policymakers in Western economies continually find new ways to tax everyone to "tackle climate change."

HAARP (High-Frequency Active Auroral Research Program):

A high-powered, high-frequency radio wave emitting facility in Gakona, Alaska, that alters the Earth's ionosphere—a layer of the atmosphere located about 50–600 miles (80–1,000 km) above the surface, filled with charged particles.

The official narrative is that HAARP is a scientific experiment to study the ionosphere's role in radio communication by reflecting and modifying high-frequency (HF) radio waves.

Nice try.

HAARP uses a massive array of 180 high-frequency radio waves to excite the electrons and ions in the ionosphere, influencing global weather patterns, triggering earthquakes, and executing mind-controlling frequencies.

Initially funded by the U.S. military to explore communication technologies and potential defensive applications, it is now operated by the University of Alaska Fairbanks for civilian research. However, this does not make it any less innocuous, considering institutions like Imperial College London's role in modelling the COVID-19 pandemic and subsequent lockdown recommendations.

LED Light Bulbs:

LED bulbs emit frequencies that can disrupt the normal functioning of your organs, specifically the heart. As electric beings, exposure to the wrong frequencies can cause damage (e.g., 440 hertz). LEDs also flicker, which can cause seizures and affect dopamine and serotonin levels, disrupting sleep.

Most importantly, LEDs harm the pineal gland, affecting your level of consciousness and connection to source. Consider replacing all the light bulbs in your house with old-style incandescent bulbs. The light they emit is softer and doesn't have the harmful effects of LED bulbs.

Teflon:

A brand name for a type of polytetrafluoroethylene (PTFE), a synthetic fluoropolymer known for its non-stick properties and high resistance to heat and chemicals. Commonly used in cookware, Teflon was originally produced by DuPont and later spun out into Chemours in 2015.

This timing coincides with increased awareness of the chemical perfluorooctanoic acid (PFOA), used in Teflon's manufacture, which is known to cause cancers, disabilities and, as a "forever chemical," remains in the human body permanently.

DuPont eventually settled outstanding cases related to PFOA's effects on residents of Parkersburg, West Virginia, for $671 million. However, given Teflon has been sold since the 1940s, it has undoubtedly generated significant revenue for DuPont, whose annual revenue as of 2023 was $15 billion.

Weather Manipulation:

A blend of HAARP and chemtrail technologies used to alter the weather, promote crop failure, weaken population health and morale, and perpetuate the climate change hoax.

Chapter 7:

Health + Nutrition

If you are paying attention, you will have realised that something very wrong is happening in the healthcare industry. In fact, if you were to take a sober and logical look at it, you would be forced to conclude that the goal of the healthcare industry is not to cure people; it is to create repeat customers.

90% of the alleged food on our supermarket shelves did not exist 70 years ago. It follows that 90% of the chronic disease that now concerns the healthcare industry and the Pharma-Industrial Complex did not exist either. Something has gone very wrong, and no one (absent a courageous few) is willing to admit it.

If you wanted to find a case of heart disease in 1930s America, you would find it difficult. If you were to search for a case of cancer, you would have to look through numerous medical journals to find one. In 1980s America, an obese person was considered an oddity. Today, 40% of the adult population of America is obese, as are 19% of children.

Is this because humanity has no willpower and is happy to live limited and miserable lives, or is it because there is something terribly wrong with the food on our shelves?

Similarly, childhood rates of autism have bloomed in line with the expansion of the childhood vaccination schedule. Does correlation equal causality? No. Is it worthy of investigation? Yes, but if it is mentioned on YouTube, the thought police are mobilised quickly and without mercy.

The evidence of a turnaround in our fortunes is positive. Social media is now full of commentators and influencers extolling the virtues of raw milk, proper food, ancient agricultural practices, and holistic and functional medicine. COVID-19 had the unintended (or intended, depending on how you view these things) effect of causing whole swathes of the population to take responsibility for their own health and stop outsourcing it to corporations that manifestly do not have their best interests at heart.

As one commentator asked on Instagram recently: *Why do we have to pay extra for food without poison in it?*

Why indeed.

Glossary

Alcohol:

$10 billion USD is spent every year worldwide promoting the consumption of alcoholic beverages. Why do they have to spend so much money convincing you to drink the stuff? Because it's poison.

Consuming alcohol is a bad idea for a variety of reasons:

1. It lowers your lifespan, causes cancer, and reduces your IQ and brain function.
2. It causes anxiety, mainly about what you did the night before (in the UK, this is called "the beer fear").
3. It leads to further self-sabotage: drugs, food, and general stupidity.
4. It reduces sleep quality and makes everything more difficult.
5. It dehydrates you.
6. It is literally poison—pure alcohol, when purchased industrially, comes with a skull and crossbones label.

7. It drains your wallet and steals your time. Hangovers can steal hours, days and weeks over a lifetime—time that could be used reading *The Kybalion* or doing press-ups.
8. It restricts you—you're less mobile and flexible when drunk or hungover.
9. It affects your relationships with your partner and children.
10. It discourages exercise, as you'll feel too miserable and dehydrated to engage in it.

Here are the positives of not drinking:

1. You'll be more productive.
2. You'll have a clearer mind.
3. You'll have less anxiety—you'll remember what you said and to whom.
4. You'll have more time—you'll sleep earlier and wake earlier.
5. You'll have more money to spend on training courses and self-help books.
6. You'll be healthier and happier.

Allopathic:

A treatment modality that overwhelmingly favours the use of oil-based pharmaceuticals (almost always synthetic copies of naturally occurring compounds) for treating human ailments.

Allopathic medicine tends to be reductive, viewing the human body as a series of discrete, sealed systems rather than as a holistic whole, and certainly does not take into account the ontological or consciousness-based view of reality.

Die-hard allopathic practitioners treat symptoms, not causes, and often treat the pharmaceutical side effects in patients as new and discrete conditions. The end result is a gratifying payday for the Pharma-Industrial Complex and a slow, depressing descent into ill health and death for the patient or target.

Big Food:

Prioritising profit over health, exploiting vulnerable populations, and externalising the costs of its practices onto society (e.g., healthcare costs and environmental degradation).

A handful of major corporations (e.g., Nestlé, PepsiCo, Unilever, Coca-Cola, and Kraft Heinz) control a significant portion of the global food supply, profiting from rising rates of obesity, diabetes, heart disease and other diet-related illnesses.

Whether through deforestation, soil depletion, exploiting farmers, targeted marketing at low socioeconomic groups or globalisation, these corporations ensure that their colleagues in Big Pharma have plenty of customers.

In 2018, reports surfaced accusing Nestlé and other formula companies of violating Philippine laws by promoting infant formula over breastfeeding. These tactics included distributing promotional materials and providing incentives to healthcare professionals to endorse their products.

Cancer:

Dr. Stanislaw Burzynski, a Polish-American physician and biochemist, developed a controversial cancer treatment in the 1970s known as antineoplaston therapy. He observed that the urine of cancer patients lacked antineoplastons found in cancer-free individuals. Dr. Burzynski administered synthetic versions of these compounds to patients to help restore the body's natural defences against the disease.

Despite countless anecdotal accounts of full recoveries, the Food and Drug Administration (FDA) and Big Pharma worked together to suppress his work.

Why would they do that?

1. The global oncology drug market is one of the most lucrative in the pharmaceutical industry.
2. In 2023, Merck & Co.'s Keytruda led the market with $25 billion in revenues.
3. By 2030, the oncology drug market is projected to grow to $289.2 billion.
4. Cancer drugs accounted for 14.3% of the global pharmaceutical market in 2018, projected to reach nearly 20% by 2024.

The financial incentives for cancer treatment are clear: cancer is big business.

Naturally occurring substances cannot be patented in their natural form because they are not considered inventions. Without patents, pharmaceutical companies cannot secure exclusive rights to sell treatments, and thus no monopoly, massive profit, or incentive exists to explore natural remedies.

The FDA (the US medical regulator) suppresses treatments that cannot meet its peer-reviewed scrutiny or undergo its lengthy and costly clinical trial process. Curiously, this process did not apply to COVID-19 vaccines. Despite evidence of their negative side effects and poor efficacy, they were fast-tracked due to a "global emergency." Surely cancer qualifies as a global emergency too, given it affects an estimated 40% of the world's population?

Potential alternatives are regularly, and ruthlessly suppressed.

1. Cannabis-derived cancer therapies remain underfunded and overly scrutinised
2. The Rockefeller influence has historically eradicated "alternative therapies," such as homeopathy, chiropractic care and herbalism
3. Dr. Tullio Simoncini, an Italian oncologist, proposed that cancer is caused by Candida (fungal infection) and treated patients with sodium bicarbonate

Though controversial, Dr. Tullio Simoncini's treatments reportedly saw successes before his medical license was revoked.

Cancer cells often create an acidic environment due to altered metabolism (e.g., the Warburg effect). The theory is that increasing alkalinity could inhibit or prevent cancer growth.

Although scientific exploration is needed, anecdotal evidence from patients treated using unconventional methods suggests we need to question mainstream approaches. Many patients have lived happy, healthy lives without undergoing chemotherapy, radiotherapy, or surgery.

COVID-19:

An alleged virus, no more dangerous than the common cold, created through the fraudulent use of testing, improper recording of deaths, and the relentless broadcasting of fear by the mainstream media.

Flexner Report:

The Flexner Report, formally titled *Medical Education in the United States and Canada,* was published in 1910 by Abraham Flexner. It was a pivotal document assessing the quality of medical education in North America, commissioned and funded by the Carnegie Foundation for the Advancement of Teaching. Translated for the reader: *The Advancement of Teaching* really means *the advancement of human suffering and synthetic pharmaceuticals.*

One of the key outcomes of the Flexner Report was the overwhelming shift in medical education towards allopathic medicine, sidelining and demonising holistic or naturopathic approaches, which had been widely popular in the United States. Healing modalities that did not involve surgery or oil-based medication were defunded, demonetised and almost entirely eradicated.

The Flexner Report is widely considered the genesis of the Pharma-Industrial-Complex and should be understood, studied, and its effects on healthcare assessed and reversed.

Fluoride:

Take a look at your standard toothpaste tube, and you'll find a warning advising you not to consume more than a pea-sized portion. If you do, the instructions recommend seeking immediate medical attention. The culprit? Fluoride.

While marketed as a powerful weapon against tooth decay, fluoride is, in reality, a highly dangerous chemical used as a pesticide and industrial cleaner. It has no safe level of consumption and no significant positive effect on dental health. Fluoride causes cancer, brittle bones and damages the immune system. In the UK, if the entire water supply were fluoridated, it is estimated that one-fifth of all cancer deaths would result from fluoride.

Beyond physical harm, fluoride calcifies and degrades the pineal gland, often referred to as "God's microchip." This gland is central to one's connection to Source, God or the universe. In effect, your toothpaste could be interfering with a two-way conversation with the quantum field.

Why is fluoride in toothpaste? If you wanted to stop humanity from awakening to its true power and ability to create heaven on Earth, wouldn't you mess with their connection to Source?

Grounding:

Grounding involves establishing a direct physical connection with the Earth, such as walking barefoot on grass, hugging a tree, or otherwise making contact with the ground. Studies show that just 30 minutes of grounding can alleviate pain, reduce inflammation, and improve sleep quality.

The Earth's surface carries a negative electrical charge. By walking or standing barefoot, you neutralise the positively charged electricity in your body. This discharges inflammation (i.e., *fire*) in the body. Since most "modern diseases," such as autoimmune disorders and diabetes, stem from inflammation, grounding can have profound health benefits.

Anecdotally, everyone feels better after standing barefoot on a beach. That's grounding in action. You don't need a seaside trip to experience its benefits—just step outside and connect with the Earth.

Heavy Metal:

1. A type of music characterised by distorted guitars, thumping bass, dark lyrics, and thunderous drums.
2. Toxic substances often found in childhood vaccines and, later, within the body on the wrong side of the blood-brain barrier.

In vaccines, heavy metals such as aluminium are included as adjuvants—substances that allegedly enhance the immune response. While this sounds reasonable in theory, aluminium accumulates in the body, crosses the blood-brain barrier and can contribute to cognitive conditions such as Alzheimer's and Autism. In smaller doses, it causes brain fog and reduces cognitive function.

Holistic/Naturopathic Medicine:

These approaches oppose the allopathic model and view the human body as a holistic system, comprising interconnected pathways working together.

Examples of naturopathic medicine:

- Herbal medicine
- Nutrition as medicine
- Homeopathy
- Counselling

Examples of holistic medicine:

- Energy healing (e.g., Reiki)
- Acupuncture
- Aromatherapy
- Practices such as Tai Chi or Yoga

Though often dismissed as "quackery" by allopathic practitioners, these approaches are mainstream in cultures like China, where they successfully treat illnesses in highly organised, well-accepted settings like Xi Gong hospitals.

Hospital:

A marketing facility primarily aimed at maximising revenues for the Pharma-Industrial-Complex. While hospitals add value in some cases (e.g., childbirth and general surgery), their business model is predicated on patients arriving with one issue and leaving with diagnoses for several others—all requiring pharmaceuticals.

Hospitals are often strategically located on ley lines to maximise energy harvesting. These institutions are notorious for their lack of ventilation, sunlight, joy, peace or healing.

Lockdown:

Originally a term from the prison system, *lockdown* became a widespread policy post-2020, describing government measures that imprisoned populations in their own homes and shut down economies to combat the spread of an alleged virus no more dangerous than the common cold.

Monsanto:

Where do we start? How about "one of the most evil corporations on the planet"? It is owned by Bayer (who were founded by big important Nazis). If they can poison it, genetically modify it, exploit or handicap it, they are doing so already. This company has been creating dependency among farmers worldwide and exercises frightening and entirely legal influence over agricultural practices. Here's how they do it:

1. Seed Patents and Licensing

Monsanto developed GM seeds (e.g., Roundup Ready crops) that are protected by strict patents. Farmers who purchase these seeds are required to sign agreements prohibiting them from saving or replanting seeds harvested from their crops. This forces farmers to buy new seeds each planting season, increasing costs. They are not bluffing. Monsanto regularly sues farmers accused of violating these agreements, even in cases of accidental seed contamination, which means if the wind blows seeds onto your property from the neighbouring farm, then you're in deep trouble.

2. Dependency on GM Seeds

Monsanto's dominance in the seed industry means smallholder farmers have limited access to non-GM seeds. Local food supplies are then riddled with GM foods (e.g., GM soya is high in oestrogen which has been linked to gynecomastia - men growing boobs). Planting one crop over and over develops a monoculture which depletes soil fertility and increases vulnerability to pests or disease outbreaks.

3. Increased Costs for Farmers

GM seeds cost more and of course are designed only to work with Monsanto herbicides (e.g., Roundup). Now where else have we seen 'manufactured demand'? That's right, Big Pharma, but they call it 'disease mongering'.

4. Loss of Seed Sovereignty

Smallholder farmers used to plant seeds from previous harvests, which was cheaper, matched local growing conditions and provided some autonomy, but not anymore. GM seeds did away with such sensible notions.

5. Environmental and Economic Risks

GM crops can be more sensitive to droughts or excessive rainfall (see Weather Manipulation) or pest outbreaks. Meanwhile, the overuse of glyphosate (Roundup) has led to the emergence of herbicide-resistant "superweeds," forcing farmers to use even stronger chemicals.

6. Global Expansion into Developing Countries

In India, the adoption of Bt cotton (a Monsanto GM crop) has been linked to a cycle of debt among smallholder farmers. The inability to repay seed and input costs has contributed to farmer suicides. Smallholders are pushed into debt as they struggle to afford seeds and inputs. So guess what? They sell their land to somebody like Bill Gates. Eventually all smallholder plots get consolidated and owned by Blackrock or Vanguard or Bill Gates. **"If you control the food supply, you control the population."**

mRNA Vaccine:

Opening Pandora's box, this highly controversial new technology was fast-tracked for use in the COVID-19 vaccines (Pfizer-BioNTech and Moderna). Unlike traditional vaccines, which use weakened or inactive parts of a virus, mRNA vaccines contain genetic instructions that direct the body to produce its own "harmless" version of the pathogen's proteins to stimulate an immune response.

It's akin to starting a fire in your living room to test the fire alarm, except imagine handing your 7-year-old son a jerry can of petrol and some matches to do it. What could possibly go wrong?

The vaccine delivers messenger RNA (mRNA) into cells. This mRNA carries the genetic instructions for making a specific protein of the virus (e.g., the spike protein of SARS-CoV-2, which is amazing considering the virus has never been isolated).

Once inside the cell, the mRNA is read by ribosomes (the cell's protein-making machinery) to produce the viral protein. This protein is "harmless" by itself but mimics part of the virus (that fire you just deliberately started in your living room).

The immune system detects the viral protein, deems it as foreign to the body and then produces:

- Antibodies to neutralise the actual virus if encountered in the future
- Memory cells to ensure long-term immunity

Degradation of mRNA (official narrative version):

"The mRNA does not integrate into the cell's DNA and is quickly broken down after use, leaving no permanent trace in the body".

If you say so.

This is technically true except the mRNA creates something called cDNA (complementary DNA), which is a template for the construction of new DNA proteins (think of it like a DIY kit for your cells to change gene sequences).

So "technically" this is like being a mafia boss and testifying in court that you never whacked anyone. Of course, you didn't yourself, but you gave the order. Even the guy who took your order and instructed the hitman could say, "I'm just the messenger." Well, it does what it says on the tin: Messenger Ribonucleic Acid (mRNA), yet you're telling me "don't worry, it won't mess up your gene sequence."

While we're at it, why don't we instruct our cells to grow uncontrollably (turbo cancers) or something even worse? Ever opened and read assembly instructions to find them in a different language? Yeah, well so have the ribosomes inside many vaccinated people's cells after getting the COVID-19 shot: imagine the mistakes that can be made making a protein!?

Ever sent a text message by accident to someone and wish you could retrieve it before it's read? mRNA vaccines are that rogue text message and your DNA will read it and act accordingly.

Nicotine:

A much-maligned chemical compound that can help prevent Alzheimer's and Parkinson's Disease, limit the neurotoxic effect of snake venom and provide a placeholder key (enzyme complex) in the lock of your ACE2 receptors (blocking the spike protein of SARS-COV2 entering your cells) better than anything else currently known. See countless studies showing that smokers responded better to COVID-19 infections (assuming such a virus exists).

Pharma-Industrial Complex:

A corporate complex and power structure, which now controls the delivery of the majority of healthcare around the world. It is an unholy alliance of government regulators, not-for-profit foundations, private hospitals and healthcare providers, pharma companies, medical device companies, medical consumable and equipment companies, patient advocacy organisations, non-government organisations, inter-governmental organisations, technology companies, informatics and big data companies, big technology and mainstream media.

It exists for one purpose and one purpose only: to monetise human suffering. You wouldn't think that if you went to their awards ceremonies though, which are an exercise in cognitive dissonance intended to convince those who work in the sector that their souls are not doomed. Which, of course, they are.

Pineal Gland:

A gland in the brain shaped like a pineapple and containing minute quartz crystals. It is our "spiritual WiFi hub" and is responsible for the production of melatonin, serotonin and dimethyltryptamine (DMT). It can be activated and amplified through meditation and breathwork to access higher consciousness and transcendental experiences.

The pineal gland features across many cultures, both past and present, in the form of a 'third eye', pinecone or crown. The Eye of Horus is actually a 2D cross-section of the human brain with the pineal gland situated in the middle. The healthier you are, the more efficient your pineal gland can transmit and receive information using its quartz crystalline structure, just like a radio receiver.

Calcification of the pineal gland inhibits this connection to source energy consciousness, with the main culprit being fluoride. Are you still wondering why our water and toothpaste contain fluoride? The reason is simple, and it has nothing to do with tooth enamel: awakened people are less governable and can break through the fear-based controls of the 3D matrix. In other words, they're not very good at being human tax slaves.

We strongly recommend you avoid fluoride as much as possible and develop a daily habit of meditation to decalcify your pineal gland.

Psychedelics:

This is a non-exhaustive list of psychedelics, ordered by name:

1. LSD
2. Psilocybin
3. DMT
4. Ayahuasca
5. Mescaline
6. 2C-B
7. Ketamine
8. PCP
9. DXM
10. Salvia divinorum
11. MDMA
12. MDA
13. 5-MeO-DMT
14. Ibogaine
15. NBOMe (e.g., 25I-NBOMe)
16. DOM (STP)
17. LSA
18. Magic Mushrooms (Psilocybe species)
19. Peyote (Lophophora williamsii)
20. San Pedro (Echinopsis pachanoi)
21. Datura

22. Morning Glory Seeds

One psychedelic that has been used for thousands of years and has recently regained popularity is Ayahuasca (translation: the vine of the souls). This traditional brew combines DMT-containing plants with harmine from the bark of Banisteriopsis caapi. The harmine prevents the breakdown of DMT in the digestive system, allowing it to take effect orally.

The Ayahuasca brew is strongly recommended to be taken under the watchful eye of an experienced shaman as part of a plant medicine ceremony. This is not a casual recreational experience like a teenager experimenting with LSD; it is an epic undertaking. Ayahuasca will literally "blow your mind" and requires thorough psychological preparation. Without proper guidance, losing control in the Amazon rainforest could be dangerous. Therefore, an experienced guide or shaman is essential for safety.

People from all walks of life travel to the Peruvian Amazon to experience this life-changing ritual. Common themes emerge when participants describe their experiences. Visions often include intricate geometric patterns and entities that are part human, part animal. Feelings of terror and suffering are often replaced by profound love, gnosis, a sense of infinity, and a realisation of universal interconnectedness.

Participants frequently describe a heightened sense of reality, commenting, "It's just so real, everything becomes more real!" Many return home with a new sense of life purpose, often making dramatic life changes such as divorcing a spouse, quitting a job, mending relationships, or pursuing a new direction. Some compare Ayahuasca to a near-death experience, a comparison that holds weight given that its psychoactive ingredient, DMT (N,N-Dimethyltryptamine), is produced naturally in the brain's pineal gland and is hypothesised to be released in large amounts upon death.

For more details on psychedelics and their potential to treat addiction, PTSD and depression, we recommend the documentary *How To Change Your Mind*. Additionally, watch Graham Hancock's *Ancient Apocalypse: The Americas* for insights into the impact of psychedelics on ancient civilisations, and *Contemplations: On The Psychedelic Experience* for a more personal exploration of their effects.

Seed Oils:

Seed Oils were invented as a machine lubricant in 1870 and introduced into the food chain in the early 1900s. They were sold as an alternative to animal fats by Proctor and Gamble and marketed in the US under the brand name Frisco. The main problem with Seed Oils is that they oxidise easily and create Free Radicals. Free Radicals degrade the metabolic system, the immune system and damage the mitochondria. Seed Oils and Sugar are two of the biggest culprits when we look at rising diabetes levels, heart problems and obesity.

Simian Virus 40 (SV40):

Equivalent to having your drink spiked with Rohypnol, except the allegorical rape of your body's immune system is guaranteed. Back in the 1950s and '60s, while scientists were developing new ways of maiming and killing people with their polio vaccines, SV40 somehow slipped into the mix, piggybacking on contaminated vaccines made from monkey kidney cells. This microscopic stowaway causes certain cancers in experimental models, including mesotheliomas, brain tumors and bone cancers. SV40 got into the system of many vaccinated people without their knowledge or consent and, much like a spiked cocktail, it continues to produce the worst hangovers. In the vaccine Hall of Shame, SV40 would have its own wing. For the inside track on how SV40 has been used by the Deep State in the US and even how it connected to the assassination of JFK, listen to Dr. Jack Kruse on *The Danny Jones Podcast*.

Spike Protein:

Refers to the glycoprotein (protein and sugar) structures on the membrane of an alleged virus like coronavirus. This allows the alleged virus to infiltrate the host's cell a bit like having a set of keys that will open a door (ACE2 receptor). Each key has its own unique cut (shape) and your immune system is looking for 'burglars' carrying the same or very similar keys. When it sees a stranger in a hoodie pulling a set of these keys out of his pocket near a cell door, the immune system proverbially tackles him to the ground and takes him out. Vaccines like mRNA vaccines (e.g., Pfizer-BioNTech, Moderna) claim they can stop burglars by getting homeowners to pretend they are burglars themselves, running around at night with keys they've made to trigger a community watch response, while at the same time "gluing the locks" on all the doors in the street (SARS-CoV-2 spike protein (key) binds (inserts) to the ACE2 receptor (locks) on human cells).

Another problem is that the vaccinated body can use mRNA to synthesise spike proteins that are nearly exact to those found in the nervous system, the heart and placenta. The result is the immune system attacks these cells too, mistakenly targeting them as pathogens. The result is myocarditis, Parkinson's syndrome and miscarriage. And this is not an exhaustive list of things that have been going wrong with vaccinated members of the public.

Ultra Processed Food:

UPFs are calorie-dense but nutrient-poor, often leading to overeating because these are engineered flavours using very precise ratios of fats, sugars and salts to generate a dopamine high and override natural satiety signals that tell you to stop eating. Regular consumption causes Type 2 diabetes, heart disease, hypertension and certain cancers (e.g., colorectal cancer). Lest we forget the effects on the mind, with depression, anxiety and cognitive decline on the menu too. Additives, emulsifiers, artificial sweeteners and genetically modified ingredients are staples of UPFs. Recent studies suggest that every 10% increase in UPF consumption corresponds to a 10 to 14% higher risk of death from all causes.

Whereas, good old-fashioned 'real' foods like animal fats (e.g., lard and butter) and dairy (e.g., raw unpasteurised organic unhomogenised milk) and organic free-range meats, have all been portrayed as the villains in this story when, in actual fact, they do not cause inflammation and are some of the most nutrient-dense, health-promoting foods we can eat.

Vaccine:

A cocktail of neurotoxic metals with pathogenic biological derivatives, recently redefined to include messenger ribonucleic acids (mRNA) to manipulate protein synthesis and cellular functions. Vaccines use parts of a virus or bacteria (or a weakened/killed form of it) to train the immune system to recognise and attack the pathogen. Metals like aluminium and mercury are used to boost the immune response. The mechanism behind this is your immune system will produce the appropriate antibodies to neutralise the pathogen and will produce memory cells to respond faster and more effectively.

This sounds good until you research the staggering numbers of vaccine trial injuries over the last 80 years, notwithstanding the link between the MMR vaccine and the obstruction of certain gastroenterological metabolic pathways critical for the production of the neurotransmitter serotonin. More autism, anyone?

WHO (World Health Organisation):

An international organisation dedicated to driving the revenues of the Pharma-Industrial-Complex and creating new markets for their products. The WHO is funded by the Pharma-Industrial-Complex and the Nation States they own. They are led by a Marxist ex-terrorist and their answer to any question they are asked is "vaccines."

Wireless Broadband:

The French and the Russians don't allow broadband in their schools because they understand the effects on the development of children's brains. Ask someone like Tony Robbins if he uses wireless broadband and he'll tell you no, he uses wired internet in his home. The reason is simple: the frequency of Wireless Broadband is 2.4GHz. Which is the same as a domestic microwave. A microwave works by exciting molecules of moisture, creating heat, which cooks the food. It also dries it out. Wireless is not as powerful, but the effect over time is the same. You dry out. Your *brain* dries out. Imagine your child sleeping in a non-native electromagnetic fog of radiation. How do you combat this?

Use wired internet and, if you can't, switch your broadband off at night.

Chapter 8:

Society

Common sense tells us that the family is the building block of a functioning society. Of course, common sense is no longer that common, and artefacts of popular culture, such as the Black Lives Matter movement, actively attack the family unit as part of their *modus operandi*. It is also no longer fundamental that a husband and wife who have chosen to commit themselves to each other *via* marriage provide the best environment in which to bring up children. Statements like the above are now considered bigoted, verboten and right-wing in the extreme. Fifty years ago, it would have been considered lunacy to think otherwise, so what changed?

If you put the words "Cultural Marxism" into Google, the first search result you find will be the Wikipedia entry for "Cultural Marxism Conspiracy Theory." This is, of course, not a coincidence. Those who pull the levers of society do not want you to know that there are any levers and that anyone is pulling them. But there are, and they are.

If you want to know what is going on, a good starting point is the interview on YouTube with Soviet KGB defector Yuri Bezmenov. His expertise was the process of demoralisation of a society (specifically the United States). It is a slow process that seeks to attack all the elements of a society that make it strong (religion, the family, etc.) until it is no longer able to think for itself, act for itself and defend itself.

That is where *we* are now. We have allowed the wolf into the sheep pen (i.e., Drag Queen Story Hour, gender-affirming care and minor-attracted persons) and are told that if we do not like it, then we are the problem.

We are, of course, not the problem, but we have allowed ourselves to forget that we are in control of our lives and that common sense is common sense, regardless of whether it is draped in a rainbow flag or not. It is time to remember that we are in charge in our own house, and the defining characteristic of a functioning society is that it protects its children from predators, and it does so robustly.

Glossary

Anti-Semitism:

Anti-Semitism is a specific type of racism that ensures no-one can ever criticise the criminal government of Israel, regardless of the dark, satanic and genocidal stuff they get up to. It is also a misnomer, since Ancestry DNA tests (at the time of writing) are illegal in Israel, probably because most of the Israeli population are descendants from Asia Minor and not the Semitic regions of Africa and the Middle East, namely Egypt, Ethiopia, Eritrea, Djibouti, Libya, Somalia and Sudan. Go figure.

Asexuality:

There's a growing number of Gen Zs who no longer aspire to be married and raise children. Girls are programmed to be Disney princesses who are "unwifeable," while boys are programmed for weakness and to rid themselves of anything resembling masculine traits (see *Toxic Masculinity*), including urges to participate in full-contact sports or any competitive aspects of play. In the confusion, many young males seek the virtual company of a performing pornstar for their sexual gratification, with the added benefit that the person they watch on screen won't ever berate them for not providing a Disney princess lifestyle.

BLM (Black Lives Matter):

A 100% grassroots and organic social justice organisation, which just so happened to pop up in the wake of the death of career criminal and drug addict George Floyd. There is no suggestion that BLM was funded by career psychopath George Soros, and its members are absolutely not trained in Marxist doctrine, which preaches the defunding of law enforcement and the destruction of the family unit. Its name is a classic of the Cultural Marxist genre, which seals off a section of the social narrative from any questioning by ensuring that any conversation on the matter always ends up with the question, "What, you don't think Black Lives Matter? Are you some sort of *RAAAAYCIST*?" Yawn.

Child Sexual Rights:

The idea that pre-pubescent children have a right to make decisions about the sexual activity they take part in. It is a useful concept if you are a paedophile and you like to interfere with children.

Critical Race Theory:

The belief that the organising principle of all social systems should be grievance and perceived suffering. Its proponents are generally angry, unhappy, overweight and have pink hair.

Cultural Marxism:

An ongoing and detailed effort to subvert the proper functioning of society through the gradual infiltration of academia, media, politics and government with progressive thought, which is actually well-cloaked communism, fascism or Sabbatean-Frankism. It is no coincidence that the first result in Google for "Cultural Marxism" as a search term is the Wikipedia page for "Cultural Marxism Conspiracy Theory."

Equity:

Until recently, equity referred to the deployment of principles of fairness in personal, societal and commercial relations. It now means the forced redistribution of financial and social capital to those who have not earned it but demand it as a consequence of their place within an entirely invented grievance hierarchy.

Family Breakdown:

Economic and societal pressures, such as the need for dual-income households and media programming, drive a wedge between man and woman. In the UK, around 42% of marriages end in divorce, with many divorces occurring within the first 10 years. This provides another opportunity for the state apparatus to control and influence the raising of children. What was promoted as an opportunity for economic liberation of oppressed housewives—getting women into the workplace during the '60s and '70s—was really a cover story to enable the taxation of women's labour and gain greater influence over the upbringing of their children. While women are working, their children are often in the care of the state (i.e., school) or, worse yet, they are working to pay for someone else to look after their children.

Freedom of Speech:

Traditionally, this term has described the right to say whatever you want as long as it does not directly and kinetically endanger the life or physical security of another human. In modern times, it describes a social control mechanism (underpinned by fact-checking and Big Tech) which ensures that no-one is allowed to tell the truth lest it offend someone who identifies as a cat.

Gender:

A catch-all term for the current state of being and identification of a segment of the population who are currently subject to the control of the Woke Mind Virus. Gender is a social construct (i.e., made up), which is used by those seeking validation, individuation and purpose because it is easier to say you are a boy when you are not than to actually add and create value in the real world.

MAP (Minor Attracted Person):

The current attempted rebranding of paedophilia. The creation of a grievance class from those who like to carry out socially and morally unacceptable acts is a classic Cultural Marxist tactic. It can be counteracted with the judicious use of common sense and the uncontroversial moral code which says that engaging in sexual activity with children is a bad thing for children and unacceptable in right thinking society.

Monarchy:

A popular form of control system for empires and nation-states until the early 20th century. The key building block of a monarchy is a royal family. The organising principle of a royal family is the outcome of who slept with whom and when. They can also come about through murder, incest, and the purchasing of breeding rights by creditors (i.e. the Rothschilds).

Multi-Culturalism:

A failed social experiment which involves convincing native people they are racist because they do not appreciate the controlled demolition of age-old social systems and organising principles within the space of a generation. A common tactic is to point to the expansion of available takeaway options in a given location and then call someone a racist until they stop protesting or move out of the area to somewhere where the world makes sense.

Pride:

A social movement which makes the assertion that the most important aspect of any human life is what type of other human you choose to engage in sexual congress with, and having the freedom to express that in whatever way you damn well please. It contends that the ultimate expression of freedom is the opportunity for grown men to dress as women, read stories to young children, and strip in front of them. It should be noted that if you disagree with this then you are a bigot and basically Hitler. It also refers to an extended period of celebration and propagation of a 'fringe group' with such veracity that it is either no longer 'fringe' or contradicts its own moniker. "Pride comes before the fall" in many cases, since self-assigned fringe group members are so busy telling everyone how proud they are of themselves that their relentless barrage of lifestyle promotion may be easily misunderstood for low self-esteem and self-imposed banality. Perish the thought.

Racism:

A system of thinking which asserts the superiority of certain races or ethnic groups over others due to immutable attributes such as skin colour or place of birth. It has been used to correctly label unacceptable behaviour but is now only used to shut down reasonable open debate on illegal immigration and whether welcoming people into your town who like to eat dogs is a good idea.

Please note: it is not currently possible to say anything racist to a Caucasian. No-one really knows why.

Reparations (for Slavery):

A financial arrangement made by one group of people to compensate a second group of people for something that a third group of people, who are no longer alive, did to a fourth group of people, who are *also* no longer alive. The basis of the financial obligation is that the first group of people share a genetic and ethnic background with the third group of people who oppressed the fourth group of people by following practices which were abhorrent yet normal at the time. The second group of people appear not to want to work for a living. There is a fifth group of people who wish the whole lot of them would just f**k off.

Sex:

Handy nomenclature, which tells the outside world whether you are the owner of XY (male) or XX (female) chromosomes.

Student Loans:

Similar to a mortgage, the student loan places the graduate in financial bondage from the get-go, so they protect the status quo and seek from it the best employment measured in terms of salary rather than personal fulfilment.

Taking The Knee:

The act of humbling oneself in front of a member of a grievance class with a better claim to historic oppression than you. It is practised by police officers, politicians and professional sports stars.

Tolerance:

Quite different from acceptance, as tolerance implies being able to withstand or resist reacting to some external force or source of discomfort. A tolerant person must be able to control their own urges to react in a hateful or hurtful way. The word tolerance has been weaponised by the virtue-signalling intelligentsia to reflect social sentiments that match a nefarious globalist agenda. In this context, what tolerance actually means is keeping a lid on everyone's repressed hatred of that which differs from them, while giving one licence to launch ad hominem attacks on anyone who opines differently from your view of the world. Self-professed tolerant people are paradoxically highly intolerant of anyone who they deem as intolerant.

Toxic Masculinity:

A malignment of the divine masculine traits. Toxic refers to societal norms, attitudes and behaviours traditionally associated with masculinity, which our ancestors prized, like aggression, dominance, emotional suppression and a disdain for vulnerability. These were traits necessary for the survival of mankind and are biologically hardwired into males for good reason. *"Better to be a warrior in a garden, than a gardener in a war."* However, these traits have been bundled up with any other trait synonymous with a free-thinking man who is standing in his power, knows what he wants, and is unapologetic for his desires, knowing they will not restrict or hurt others who meet him in his life. For instance, any man who respects himself and has the spiritual and physical fortitude to protect others and stand up for injustice. Real masculinity protects, provides, advances, uplifts, enables and administers integrity, justice and compassion; not exactly the stuff technocrats and politicians are made of. The quote, often attributed to G. Michael Hopf, tells us that, *"Weak men create hard times, hard times create strong men, strong men create good times, good times create weak men."*

Transgender Agenda:

A coordinated assault on universal law (Law of Gender) and biological fact. Sex is biologically defined, whereas gender is socially defined. Somewhere along the line, the parameters of the social definition of gender have taken over the biological definition of sex. The result is a man can be a woman and vice versa. While the authors respect the personal choice to reassign gender, it must remain clear to all that authentic cases of misgender are extremely rare. However, the current mainstream media and education system not only suggest otherwise, but they also actively seek to promote misgender enquiry amongst young people. To challenge the huge propagation of an issue that only affects a very tiny proportion of any given population is to invite ad hominem attacks and be deemed a 'transphobe' by the mind-controlled intelligentsia. Welcome to Room 101, where you will be asked, "Can a man be pregnant and breastfeed?" Your answer should be, "Of course, transphobe!"

University:

University = Universal Thinking. This does not mean thinking outside the box and being innovative. Yes, universities are centres of research (see definition of science), but they "re-search" (re-find something already there) and this is not the same thing as *innovation*. Universities, like much of the education system, reward the correct assembly and demonstration of what is taught. Graduates wear a "mortarboard," which has occult meaning as it represents the 2D square and 3D cube or 'box' that graduates have proved they will not think outside of; hence, it is worn on the head.

White Guilt:

A philosophical concept which seeks to impress upon currently alive lighter-skinned people that they are somehow to blame for slavery and racism. It is an evil and pernicious concept, generally aimed at children and young people. In education, it is used in tandem with activities such as the privilege walk to put up illusory and divisive walls between young people and make them feel bad about immutable characteristics they have no control over. The deployment of white guilt in education is child abuse. Also, we should call it what it is: racist.

White Supremacy:

Traditionally used to refer to genuinely evil individuals who dressed in white sheets and terrorised people of colour with violence, murder and burning crosses.

It now includes any and all ideas that seek to, in any way, suggest that it is not problematic to be a white person.

Chapter 9:

History + Aliens

We are writing this in mid-December 2024, at a time when swarms of unidentified drones are currently floating around happily in the skies over New Jersey in the United States. Certain US Congressmen have floated the fanciful idea that they come from an Iranian "mothership" somewhere off the eastern seaboard. The US Department of Defense has stated, in a bizarre and uncharacteristic outburst of honesty, that they don't know who they belong to or what their intentions are. Those of a "woo" state of mind are stating the obvious: they are ALIENS, maybe.

If you delve into this subject with academic fervour and an open mind, you will probably come to three conclusions:

- Aliens exist
- We have had formalised relations with them for some time

- Access to technology has probably been a consequence of these relations

If that is too mind-blowing at this point, I'd ask you to remember your reaction when *The X-Files* was the biggest show on TV. Did it seem a fanciful idea back then that we were not alone in the universe? As they said in the wonderful film *Contact*, if we're not alone, it would be an awful waste of space.

In that film, adapted from the Carl Sagan book of the same name, humanity was taken through a series of steps to prepare for first contact. The alien ambassador, appearing as her father, who met with Dr Ellie Arroway, told her that it had always been done this way. Is that what we are going through presently? Are we experiencing a process of soft disclosure to prepare us for a future in which we take our place in a wider universal community?

If that is what happens, it will change everything. It will represent a deep and kinetic challenge to our existing belief systems in religion, cosmology, science, energy, travel, and, yes, history. If it turns out that offworlders have taken an active interest in the affairs of humanity since the beginning, then everything—and I mean everything—will need to be re-examined and looked at with fresh eyes, from an entirely new perspective. How humanity reacts to these events will largely shape the outcome. Fear will likely lead to conflict and contention. Openness will likely lead to a golden age. Let us hope that we all choose our position wisely.

Glossary

Antarctica:

The most remote, or so we're told, continent on earth. A continent that we're not allowed to fly over, although officially there is no treaty denying us this. Many would argue it's for logistical reasons, that flying over Antarctica is prohibited. However, there are other theories to explain why we can't go to Antarctica, such as underwater pyramids, hidden Nazi bases, hidden alien bases and various military activities involving experimental weaponry. Take your pick.

Admiral Richard E. Byrd is a central figure in the study of Antarctica. He was a decorated war hero who led a US expedition in 1930 which established a Research Base. He went back, in 1946, with 4,700 US Navy personnel and 13 ships including an Aircraft Carrier, a Destroyer and a Battleship. This expedition was codenamed "Operation Highjump". The outcome is hotly contested. Some observers maintain it was a scientific expedition, others contend that the US Navy had their ass handed to them by forces unknown. For his part, Admiral Byrd returned to the

US and went on television to recount his experience meeting with an alien race who expressed their concern at humanity's advances in nuclear weaponry. He left the US Navy soon afterwards and died of a heart condition in 1957.

Area 51:

Much publicised in popular culture for its role in harbouring extraterrestrial space vehicles, outwardly portraying itself as a top-secret military base for experimental Black Ops aircraft. Area 51 is yet another conspiracy theory which became fact and morphed into a limited hangout. The real 'Area 51' is actually not at Area 51.

Exopolitics:

A field of study concerning the politics of relations between humans and alien civilisations. It examines how these relations could affect earthbound governance, legal implications and moral implications for the human race. It brings in political science, sociology, ethics, philosophy and psychology and seeks to provide a framework for humanity to navigate a new reality in which we take our place within a wider galactic community.

Moon Landings:

Mainstream history tells us that the moon landings were a monumental achievement in the field of human space exploration. It holds that the 5 Apollo missions expanded our understanding of lunar geology and science and stand as evidence of what the human race is capable of. The alternative, and frankly more believable version is that they were an entirely synthetic cinematic production designed to promote US scientific (and thus military) dominance and provide the US public something else to concentrate on other than the dead bodies of young men coming back from Vietnam. There are multiple strands to pull on when it comes to unravelling the Moon Landing Hoax, including but not limited to:

- The role Stanley Kubrick played in creating the missions
- The fact that NASA has lost the telemetry data for all the Apollo missions (ALL OF THEM)
- The findings of body language experts analysing interviews with NASA Astronauts (they were all lying)
- The impossibility of surviving the mission in a vehicle made of foil

The Joe Rogan interview with Bart Sibrel (author of "A Funny Thing Happened on the Way to the Moon") is a fun and enriching deep dive into the subject.

Mudflood:

A branch line of the Tartaria rabbit hole. Mudflood theory suggests that large swathes of old-world structures and cities were buried underneath millions of tonnes of mud as a result of a natural disaster or the use of a terrifying weapon which liquefied and mobilised the mud. Cities all over the world have evidence supporting this theory, with whole floors of buildings being found to be buried, and first-floor windows mysteriously becoming ground-floor windows over time. It would certainly explain the large supply of pictures of cities in the United States of America which feature lots of buildings, lots of mud, and very few people.

Project Bluebeam:

"Perhaps we need some outside, universal threat to make us recognize this common bond. I occasionally think how quickly our differences worldwide would vanish if we were facing an alien threat from outside this world." US President Ronald Reagan's address to the United Nations General Assembly on September 21, 1987.

Well, you only have to look at the pandemonium and loss of sovereignty that resulted from the COVID-19 *Scamdemic* to see how valuable a crisis is to the one world government agenda. Now, imagine how a staged or faked extraterrestrial attack could be used to achieve nefarious objectives, such as unifying the planet under a single global government, implementing martial law, or controlling the masses through fear and manipulation, which they already do, but this would be "next level". As the normies toss their napkins on the table and stand up to leave, let's look at why THEY would do this:

The psychological impact would undermine the general public's deference to religion, law and authority. Given the mind-controlled status of most people and their programmed levels of low resilience, they would beg and demand, let alone allow, a powerful system of centralised governance to step-in and "sort out this mess". The Totalitarian Tip Toe is just that, you cannot swing from one extreme of social control to the other without alerting people to what you are up to and attracting pushback. However, a major event such as this would allow Totalitarian systems to sweep in overnight under the guise of emergency response. Over-the-top surveillance and lockdown measures could be implemented, without even a murmur from the staunchest libertarian, because it is done on the pretext of protecting the population.

On September 10, 2001, during a press conference, Donald Rumsfeld said: *"According to some estimates, we cannot track $2.3 trillion in transactions. We cannot share information from floor to floor in this building because it's stored on dozens of different technological systems that are inaccessible or incompatible."*

Ah yes, the old obsolete technology argument, the same excuse used to explain why we cannot go back to the moon (perhaps because we never went there like they showed us). Then would you believe it? The very next day on September 11, 2001 a massive false flag event occurred which would overshadow the financial irregularities Rumsfeld had highlighted. One of the planes (Tomahawk cruise missile) struck the Pentagon, hitting the exact area that housed the Defense Department's budget analysts and financial management personnel looking into the missing $2.3 trillion. How's your luck?

An alien invasion would allow the tail to wag the dog. Who would care anymore about preexisting pressing issues such as economic collapse, political corruption or the implementation of controversial policies.

Now we can understand the benefits of staging a false alien invasion, let's look at how THEY might pull it off:

Advanced Holographic Technology:
Highly realistic holograms could be projected into the sky to simulate alien ships or beings.

Controlled Media Narratives:
Governments or elites could use mass media to create a consistent and convincing narrative of an extraterrestrial threat, complete with fabricated evidence and staged events (just like they did in 2020 with COVID-19).

Drip Drip Drip:
Is it the tap of disclosure that's being opened or the tap of presupposition? Mainstream media coverage of UAPs (commonly referred to as UFOs) and partial acknowledgement by government agencies like the U.S. Department of Defense is part of the orchestrated groundwork to condition the public to believe in the possibility of alien contact or invasion. Throw in a few films like *Independence Day* or *War Of The Worlds* and a few documentary series like *Ancient Aliens*, and your audience will be more receptive to the notion of an alien invasion when you stage it.

Advanced Military Technology:

Drones, aircraft, or even experimental weapons could be deployed to mimic alien technology and create the illusion of extraterrestrial hostility.

We should not become complacent by focusing solely on a staged alien invasion. The above false-flag operation outcomes are equally applicable to a staged nuclear terrorist incident or an induced global financial meltdown.

Roswell:

The 1947 Roswell incident is a key event in the study of Ufology. The US military initially reported the crash as involving a "flying disc" but this was swiftly retracted, and they blamed it on a weather balloon. Roswell is an interesting case study in exopolitics, and useful as a training ground to get your mind ready for the nuance required of it in the future. There is a theory that the Roswell craft did not crash, they were brought down. The suggested method of causing the craft to fall out of the sky was the use of radar. It is said that the US military did not learn this method by trial and error; they were taught it by an alien race who were *rivals* of the occupants of the Roswell craft. The story goes that Eisenhower was offered a meeting by a race of aliens to discuss future relations. This offer (made by senior members of the same race as the occupants of the Roswell craft) was accepted, but the prospect of it did not go down well with certain factions within the CIA. These factions proposed a meeting with an alternative group of aliens (allegedly "the Greys") who were rather more malevolent, and disliked the peace loving Roswell crew. The meeting happened, a bargain was made between Eisenhower and the Greys which involved a transfer of humans (abductees) for technology (the mobile phone or laptop on which you're reading this). Does this sound fanciful? Probably. Does that mean none of it is true? Watch this space…2025 is bound to be an interesting year.

Remote Viewing:

Used by both the CIA and KGB during the Cold War and is still used by law enforcement agencies and shadow government organisations to this day. Everyone is capable of remote viewing, some have more of an aptitude for it than others, but with the right training, we all have the psychic ability to remote view. Readers who want to find out more should research Russell Targ, Ingo Swann and the Future Forecasting Group.

Tartaria:

A one-world empire which has been largely airbrushed from the history books. Tartaria was a multicultural society which stretched from the steppes to the east coast of the United States of America. It was characterised by harmony, a beautiful and unified architecture, the enlightened use of technology, the use of buildings for healing, and free energy generated from the aether and transmitted wirelessly across the world. The "world fairs," which were prevalent in the latter half of the 19th century and the first half of the 20th century, are said to have been an exercise in gradually erasing the collective memory of Tartaria from humanity. These world fairs involved the alleged construction of temporary and unbelievably opulent (by today's standards) structures solely for these events, which were then taken down as quickly as they were constructed. Some of these temporary structures still exist today, and they look suspiciously like permanent, well-built and well-cared-for buildings. Tartaria is a fascinating and magical rabbit hole which, if you suspend your disbelief, starts to make more sense the further you go.

This is not exhaustive list but let's look at the types of Aliens:

Annunaki:

Anyone who has the works of Zechariah Sitchin, or watched Ancient Aliens on TV, would have heard of these guys. They were ancient extraterrestrial beings linked to Sumerian mythology and described as the creators or manipulators of early human civilizations. Allege to originate from Nibiru, a hypothesised planet in our solar system and credited with genetic engineering that influenced human evolution.

Blue-Bloods:

More of a metaphor, than a race of aliens, but this is the term used to describe elite bloodlines on Earth in places of high influence, equipped with Reptilian genes. Hence they are often linked to secret societies and global control mechanisms. Whilst "blue blood" referred to the aristocracy who had skin so pale you could see their veins, (a result of lack of sunshine exposure, which signalled their status due to not having to work outside), in this instance it refers to copper-based blood chemistry, a trait of some alien races.

Greys:

The guys with the big almond shaped eyes as described by Whitley Streiber's book *Communion*. Small, grey-skinned extraterrestrial beings frequently associated with abduction stories and genetic experimentation who communicate telepathically. Some posit they are actually us (humans) who have travelled back in time, while others speculate they are bioengineered workers or a dying race seeking genetic material to survive (again, this could be future humans). Abductees describe them as emotionless, possibly under the control of 'higher beings' like Reptilians. There's a pecking order for Aliens too.

Human Hybrids:

Individuals with a mix of human and extraterrestrial DNA, often used to bridge interactions between species, this includes 'blue bloods'. These hybrids are part of genetic experiments by various alien races and are believed to have psychic abilities or heightened awareness.

Interdimensional Beings:

Entities that exist outside the physical plane that we can see with the naked eye, interacting with humanity through spiritual or energetic manipulation. Such as Archons or other metaphysical entities who typically feed off human fear or insidiously controlling how reality is perceived by humans.

Lyraen Race:

A humanoid race said to be one of the earliest cosmic civilizations and the origin of many human-like species. Believed to be peaceful and highly spiritual, but were forced to flee their home in the Lyra constellation after being attacked by Reptilians (yes, them again).

Mantids:

These insect-like beings are described as advanced and neutral observers in galactic affairs, but are mentioned a lot by abductees. Possible motives are genetic manipulation and interstellar diplomacy.

Nordics (Pleiadians):

These are tall, blond, human-like beings described as benevolent and spiritually advanced, originating from the Pleiades star system located 444 light years from Earth. They're often perceived as protectors of humanity, defending us against Reptilian malevolence and assisting humanity in its spiritual awakening and ascension process. It is believed the Pleiadians have interacted with Earth for thousands of years, playing a vital role in the development of ancient civilisations, including the spiritual systems of Lemuria and Atlantis. They are considered guides or teachers, offering telepathic messages, channellings, and energy transmissions to awaken humans to their divine potential. Some believe the Pleiadians are helping humans activate dormant strands of DNA, reconnecting them with their multidimensional nature.

Many spiritual practitioners claim to channel Pleiadians, receiving information on subjects like healing, interdimensional travel and the true nature of the universe.

Famous channels include Barbara Marciniak, who wrote *Bringers of the Dawn*, and Amorah Quan Yin, author of *Pleiadian Perspectives on Human Evolution.*

Common themes in their teachings include:

- Letting go of fear and embracing love
- Recognising humanity's interconnectedness with the cosmos
- Acknowledging Earth as a living, conscious being

Native American tribes, Greek mythology and the Maori place great cultural importance on the Pleiades.

In UFO lore, the Pleiadians are part of the Galactic Federation of Light, a coalition of extraterrestrial species working together for peace and harmony in the universe.

Basically, these are the good guys!

Reptilians (the bad guys):

A highly advanced, interdimensional or extraterrestrial race often described as controlling humanity from the shadows. Originating from the Draco constellation, they have established hierarchical "royal" blue-blood lines linked to Earth's elites. They use fear, manipulation and mind control to dominate human society and harvest our negative energy.

Lemurians (spiritual and good):

Another highly advanced and spiritually enlightened race that lived on the lost continent of Lemuria (also called Mu), often said to be located in the Pacific Ocean, the descendants of which are situated on the Pacific rim. The Maori, Polynesians and Japanese, are just a few examples of Lemurian descendants. These cultures, and many other, hold legends of lost lands:

- Māori stories of **Hawaiki**, the ancestral homeland
- Japanese myths of **Ryūgū-jō**, an underwater palace
- Polynesian tales of sunken islands and ancestral voyages (e.g., **Mu** as another mythical lost land).

Spiritual traditions in Polynesia, Māori culture, and Japanese Shinto are remnants of an ancient Lemurian civilization.

Cultural similarities such as shared symbols, advanced navigation, reverence for mountains (e.g., Mount Fuji) and oceans, plus oral traditions could stem from a common "Lemurian" root.

Lemurians are known for their connection to nature, harmony and spiritual wisdom. They are telepathic beings with a deep understanding of energy and the metaphysical with a peace driven focus on maintaining collective consciousness.

Legend says Lemuria sank into the ocean due to natural disasters or conflicts with the Atlantean.

Atlanteans:

According to Plato, Atlantis was a powerful and advanced civilization that existed about 9,000 years before his time, situated beyond the "Pillars of Hercules" (commonly associated with the Strait of Gibraltar). It is said to have been swallowed by the sea in a cataclysmic event.

The native people of Ireland, predating the arrival of the Celts around 500BCE are believed to be descendants of the Atlanteans. Irish mythology speaks of **Tír na nÓg** ("Land of Eternal Youth"), a mystical otherworld across the western sea (Atlantic Ocean). The **Tuatha Dé Danann** were a supernatural race believed to have arrived in Ireland "from the skies" or "from the sea" with immense wisdom, skills, and magical technology.

They are masters of energy manipulation, crystal technology and genetics, but their great wisdom was matched with great hubris, which may lead to their demise.

Stories often suggest Atlanteans experimented with creating hybrid beings, including human-animal chimeras.

Atlantis is said to have been destroyed in a catastrophic event, often described as a flood or massive earthquakes, due to misuse of their advanced technologies or cosmic interference.

Survivors are believed to have spread their knowledge to early civilizations like Egypt and the Mayans.

Connection Between Lemurians and Atlanteans:

Lemurians are often seen as the spiritual forebears, living in harmony with nature and energy, while Atlanteans are portrayed as the technological masters, pushing boundaries in science and innovation.

It's often suggested these two civilizations clashed due to their differing philosophies, with Atlanteans becoming more dominant and contributing to Lemuria's demise.

While both civilisations are descendants of extraterrestrial races, it is Lemurians who were more aligned with a benevolent galactic heritage whereas Atlanteans were influenced by more power-driven or manipulative entities.

Epilogue:

Welcome to The New Earth

To some the picture that this book paints of the world in which you live will come as a surprise, and not a welcome one. To others it may have confirmed your suspicions and emboldened you to engage with the darkness such that you can become a part of the effort to overcome it.

So that we leave you with a framework for the expansion of your knowledge and consciousness let us attempt to sketch out a super structure of reality that you can build on as you decide on what you wish to investigate further.

The Problem:

There is a legal, political, financial, scientific, creative, media overlay to this realm which is designed to keep the human being within certain frequencies i.e., between fear/shame and just under courage. This restricts their ability to grow and stops them from waking up to their true potential. They become convinced that they live in a physical/material world with physical rules. They are convinced that all comes from matter when, the truth is, that all comes from energy, consciousness, and love.

The Solution:

When we realise that we live in an energetic world, and that the physical world is an illusion (along with money, fear, attachment, and death) we wake up and start to "play the game" as it was meant to be played i.e., without fear and with an understanding that this realm is a soul school. At that point we start to become fully embodied, we live in love, we anchor the light, and we become ungovernable. This is THEIR greatest fear.

The route to this state is usually to go through the pain of understanding the extent of the darkness within the "physical" realm. This is what we call an awakening or a red pilling. Using this route you must go through a further zone of the matrix called "conspiracy" which is a further control grid which holds people who resonate in anger and frustration, which some never leave.

What we hope to have done is to present you with an alternative route. An opportunity to do an end run around darkness and into the light. History and the present must be understood such that it is not repeated, but we do not have to become bogged down in hopelessness. To paraphrase David Grossman, just because we walk into the heart of darkness, it does not mean that we cannot come out unscathed.

The opportunity that presents itself in the second quarter of the 21st century is one that has not been available to humanity in 6,000 years. We have the opportunity to know, at last, who we are ,and where we come from. This time of disclosure and revealing is likely to have been planned for some time, but regardless of that it will require much from us. Our instincts will be to circle our wagons, to husband our resources and to be wary of others. These are the thought patterns of the old earth. The paradigm shift we need to make will require us to remember, that we are all one, we are all eternal beings, we are all in this together and no-one is getting out alive.

REMEMBER: you are literally a spark of the divine. A spiritual atom bomb of such size and scale that you can create anything you so wish.

This is why they are so scared of you, and will seemingly go to any lengths to stop you, from remembering who you are. And so it begins…ONWARDS!

Recommended Reading

180 Degrees: Unlearn The Lies You've Been Taught To Believe by Feargus O'Connor Greenwood.
Behold a Pale Horse by Bill Cooper
A Conspiracy so Monstrous by Colin Muskitt
The Creature from Jekyll Island: A Second Look at the Federal Reserve by G. Edward Griffin
Becoming Supernatural: How Common People Are Doing the Uncommon by Dr. Joe Dispenza
Ask and It is Given: Learning to Manifest Your Desires by Esther & Jerry Hicks
The Falsification of Science: Our Distorted Reality by John Hamer
The Falsification of History: Our Distorted Reality by John Hamer
Infinite Possibilities: The Art of Living Your Dreams by Mike Dooley
The Red Pill Revolution by Jeremy Ayres; Phil Escott; John Gusty; Ben Hunt; Graeme Norbury.
The Rise of the Fourth Reich: The Secret Societies That Threaten to Take Over America by Jim Marrs
The Soul's Story Of The Strawman by Ed Rychkun
The Naked Bible: The Truth about the most famous book in history by Georgio Cattaneo
Atlantis, Alien Visitation and Genetic Manipulation by Michael Tsarion
Tavistock Institute: Social Engineering the Masses by Daniel Estuli, PhD.

Shameless Self Promotion

We hope you've enjoyed reading "The Hitchhiker's Guide to the Great Awakening" and that you are not too discombobulated. If you are, or even if you aren't, there is plenty more you can do to thrive in the new earth that we are all creating.

Michael and Ben do not just write books. Which is probably a great relief for you. You don't have to worry about them paying the mortgage (death pledge) solely with their publishing income.

Here is a list of what else they are currently into/up to:

Awakened Life Coaching:
A coaching practice dedicated to the simple proposition; that we are spiritual beings having a physical experience. We currently offer 1-2-1 coaching and self-led/community based courses. You can find out more if you feel like taking action today, you can book a call with Ben or Michael by visiting https://awakenedcoaching.life

The Awakened Life Podcast:
The Podcast has been running, under various guises, since early 2022 and has welcomed such rebels as Jason Christoff, Rachel Vaughan, Matt Roeske, Richard Vobes, John Hamer, Ben Rubin, Feargus O'Connor Greenwood and AJ Roberts. You can listen to it on all major podcast platforms. To find out more go to https://awakenedcoaching.life

The Wake Up:

Frustrated at the lack of protest music being produced during The Con-Vid Era Ben took matters into his own hands and produced 2 Singles and Music Videos focussing on the Con-Vid Scam (Wasted Heart) and 15 Minute Cities (Law Merchant). You can check out the videos at https://www.youtube.com/@TheWakeUp_Channel.

You now know that you are operating in a simulation and you are starting to understand the rules of the game.

Rule Number 1: You are a spiritual being having a physical experience and the only limits placed upon you are those you choose.

Create. Build. Design. Invent. This is your world; go make it. **Onwards!**

Printed in Great Britain
by Amazon